enjoying SWIMMING and DIVING

enjoying SWIMMING and DIVING

by the Diagram Group

PADDINGTON PRESS LTD
NEW YORK & LONDON

Library of Congress Cataloging in Publication Data
Diagram Group.
   Enjoying swimming and diving.

   Includes index.
   1. Swimming.   2. Diving.   3. Aquatic sports.
I. Title.
GV837.D48 1979   797.2   78-11557
ISBN 0 7092 0149 4
ISBN 0 448 22204 3 (U.S. and Canada only)

©Diagram Visual Information Ltd.1979
All rights reserved. No part of this publication may be reproduced, stored in a retrieval system, or transmitted in any form or by any means — electronic, mechanical, photocopying, recording, or otherwise — without prior permission of the publishers.

Printed and bound in the United States.

IN THE UNITED STATES
PADDINGTON PRESS
Distributed by
GROSSET & DUNLAP

IN THE UNITED KINGDOM
PADDINGTON PRESS

IN CANADA
Distributed by
RANDOM HOUSE OF CANADA LTD.

IN SOUTHERN AFRICA
Distributed by
ERNEST STANTON (PUBLISHERS) (PTY.) LTD.

IN AUSTRALIA AND NEW ZEALAND
Distributed by
A. H. & A. W. REED

Editor	Pauline Davidson
Written by	Ann Kramer, Annabel Curtis-Jones
Copy Editors	Maureen Cartwright, Damian Grint
Art Editor	Diana C. Taylor
Artists	Alan Cheung, Stephen Clark, Brian Hewson, Richard Hummerstone, Susan Kinsey, David Lightfoot, Janos Marffy, Graham Rosewarne, Ann and Jane Robertson
Art Assistant	Ray Stevens
Picture Researchers	Enid Moore, Linda Proud
Picture Credits	Australian Information Service, London. Barnaby's Picture Library, Fox Photos, E. D. Lacey, Mansell Collection, National Film Archive/©MGM, Roger Pring, Robert Walker, The Illustrated London News
Consultants	David M. Bathurst (A.S.A.) William Barclay Keith Cornish John Noonan

Foreword

"Swimmers, take your mark . . . set . . . go!" The crack of the starting gun pierces the tense aura of the pool and ten bodies spring forward. A split second later they slap against the surface, and the furious grace of arms and legs churning through the water begins. Elsewhere in the Olympic stadium a diver mounts the high board. Steadying herself with total concentration, she glides into her approach . . . springs . . . and arches swanlike into the air before rolling into a perfect triple somersault.

For all of swimming's Olympic laurels, speed and thrilling aerobatics, one of the greatest joys is in the *doing* — that satisfying feeling of watching yourself growing confident, stronger and increasingly more graceful each time you enter the water. Once the basic techniques have been mastered, there is an endless variety of activities to engage in, all promising fun and fitness.

With step-by-step illustrations plus clear and concise explanations, ENJOYING SWIMMING AND DIVING attempts to explain the basic skills that all young watersport enthusiasts need to develop. The first section shows you how to develop confidence in the water. Next are sections explaining how to perform the major strokes and what you should know about the rules of international competition. A comprehensive section on diving is next, covering the simplest headfirst entry to the most complicated twist dives seen in the Olympics. The later sections contain valuable information on water safety, underwater swimming, surfing, water skiing, synchronized or ornamental swimming and water polo.

We would like to thank the coaches who have given us the benefit of their experience. We hope we have conveyed their advice as well as their desire to help everyone discover the joys of swimming.

Contents

8 Beginning Swimming
12 Getting used to water
14 Floating
16 Gliding
18 Basic safety
20 Lakes, rivers and seas
22 Dynamics

24 Strokes
28 Dog paddle and trudgen
30 Side and backstroke
32 The crawl
34 Front crawl
36 Breaststroke
38 Back crawl
40 Butterfly dolphin

42 Competition swimming
44 Rules
50 Events

52 Diving
56 Getting started
58 Basic dives
60 Board diving
62 Posture and exercises
64 The approach
66 The hurdle
68 Back dives
70 Reverse dives
72 Inward dives
74 Twist dives
76 Pike and tuck dives
78 Somersault dives

80 Competition diving
82 Rules

88 Underwater swimming
92 Equipment
94 Necessary skills
96 Basics
98 Maneuvers
100 Underwater signals
102 Underwater activities

104 Water safety
108 Forced entry
110 Helping yourself
112 Helping others

116 Water fun
120 Fun and games
122 Surfing
128 Windsurfing
130 Water skiing
132 Ornamental swimming

134 Water polo
136 Rules
138 Basic skills
142 Goalkeeping
144 Officials
146 Fouls

150 Training

154 Glossary

158 Index

Beginning swimming

Beginning swimming

Learning to swim is always worthwhile; it is one of the most enjoyable pastimes and also a useful safety precaution. The natural buoyancy of the body also makes swimming an ideal activity for the old or disabled who can then exercise without fear of knocks or falls endangering their health.

But before you can learn to master any of the strokes, you need to learn how to relax and overcome the very natural fear of water. In this chapter we show the preliminary steps to overcoming this fear and to feeling at home in the water.

Of course, no matter what your age, you should never try learning to swim alone. Have a swimmer there with you whether in the pool or in the sea, to give you help, encouragement, and confidence.

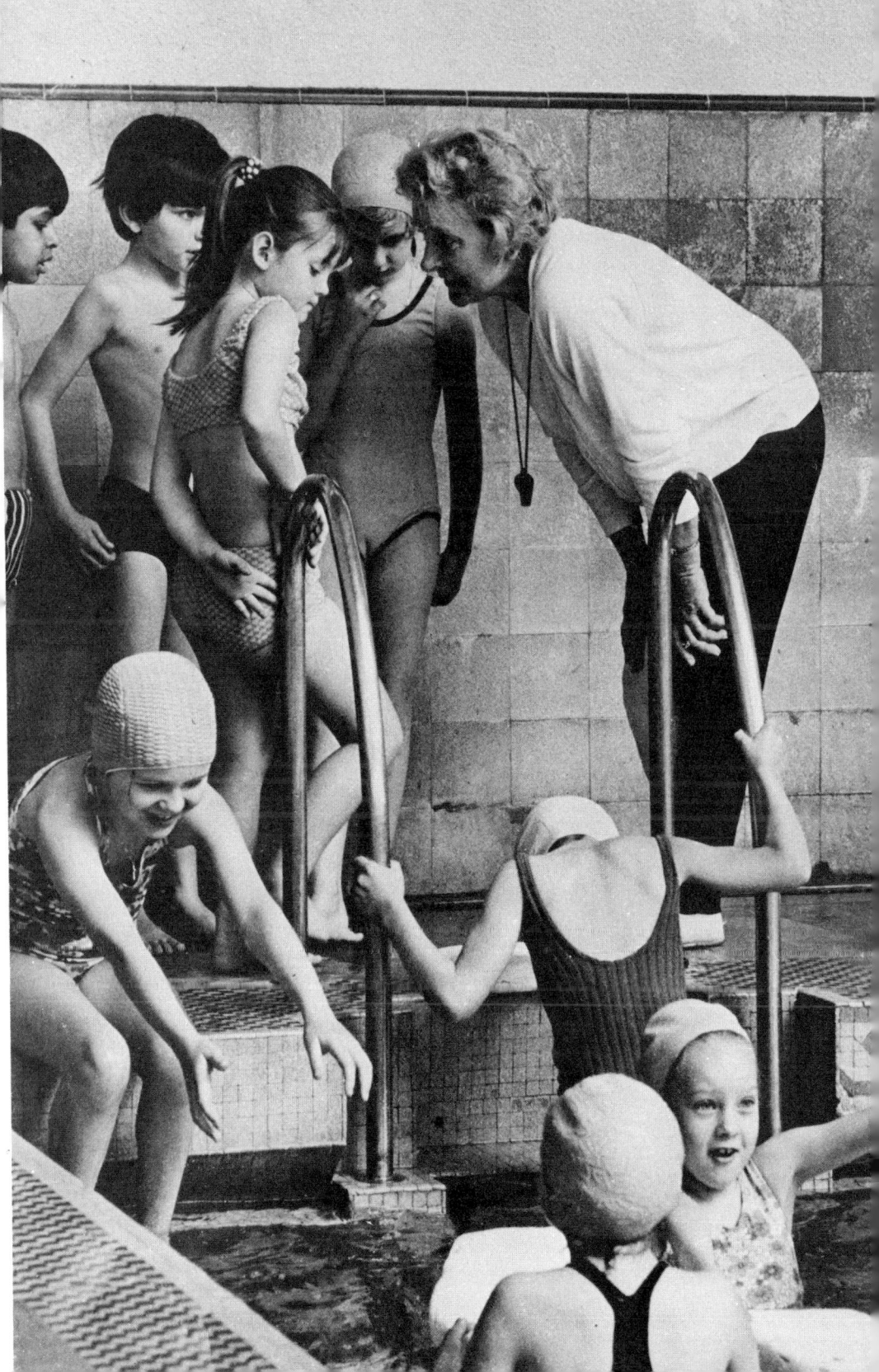

Getting used to water

equipment
When you start learning to swim all you really need is a swimsuit and perhaps a cap. You will probably also want some sort of floating aid such as a styrofoam block, rubber ring, armband, or bouyancy jacket.

confidence
Learning to swim is largely a matter of confidence; the first essential is to feel at home in the water.
1 The best way of getting into the water is as quickly as possible. Sit on the edge of the pool at the shallow end. Hold onto the bar and swing yourself around and into the water, keeping your hands on the bar all the time. Put your shoulders

right under the water and stand up. Once you have enough confidence you can jump in.

2 To start with, most people are scared of swallowing water and choking. To get over this fear, take a deep breath, bob down under the water and blow out streams of bubbles. Rise up and inhale and repeat the bubble-blowing exercise.

3 The next step is to get used to moving in water. Holding onto the rail, walk forward until you are chin-deep. Then walk back, cross the pool, and walk up the opposite side. Walk back again but this time when you are about three or four meters away, let go of the rail and walk diagonally toward the shallow end. Cross the pool and again make a diagonal crossing without holding the rail.

4 Once you are sufficiently confident you can try floating with two floats or armbands. Your shoulders should be under the water with the floats or armbands supporting your arms. Raise your knees and you will find that the water supports you easily. But until you can swim, stay in the shallow end.

Floating

breathing (above)
Breathing in water is not as difficult as it seems. Start by taking a deep breath. Bend at the waist and put your face under water. Force the air out of your lungs through your nose and mouth. Lift your face out and inhale. Also practice keeping your eyes open under water.

front float (above)
Once you have enough confidence to keep your face in the water you can try a simple front float (its unfortunate nickname is "dead man's float"). Breathe in deeply and stretch out on the water, face down. Keep relaxed and let the water do the work of supporting you.

When you have finished breathing out, come back to a standing position by bending your knees, pressing down with your arms, and lifting your head. Your feet will sink, leaving you standing upright.

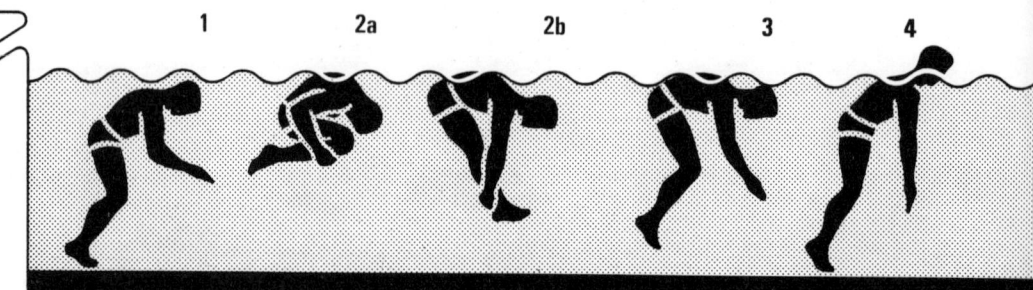

jellyfish float (above)
This is also known as the mushroom or cork float, and is one of the easiest floats to learn.
1 Start with your shoulders under water. Breathe in, submerge your face, and
2a clasp your knees with both hands so that your body is rolled into a ball with just the upper part of the back breaking the surface.
2b As a variation you can hold your ankles rather than your knees, so that you are floating in a jackknife or pike position.
3 To get back to a standing position, let go of your legs, stretching them out so that
4 your feet reach down for the bottom.

floating with a partner (above)
Try floating on your back supported by a partner. Your partner stands behind you, supporting your head with his hands. With your shoulders under water, lean back. As he moves slowly backward let your legs float upward until you are lying on your back. Keep your body straight but relaxed and keep your head well back so that your ears are just below the surface. After a few tries let your partner gradually take away his support so that you are floating on your own.

floating with the rail (above)
If you are nervous of taking your feet off the bottom, try floating with the rail. You can practice on your front or your back. Holding onto the rail, let your feet float up gently until you are lying on the surface. Kick your feet gently to remain on the surface.

back float recovery (above)
To get back into a vertical position from a back float, let your arms and legs drop. Move your arms forward, bring your knees up to your chin, and lift your head forward. This will bring you back into a standing position.

Gliding

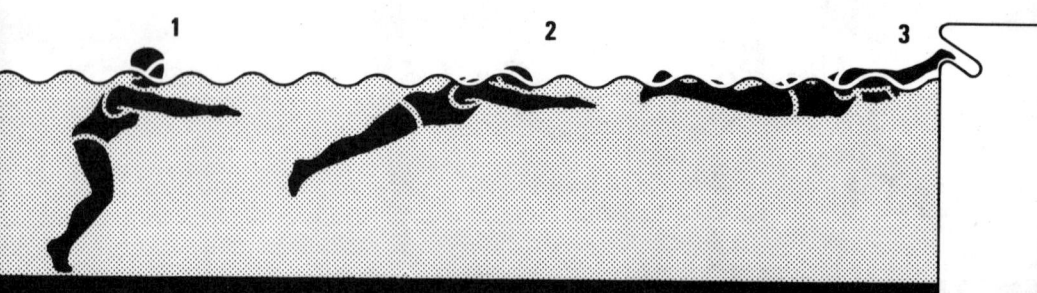

gliding (above)
Gliding is really the midway stage between floating and swimming. Basically a glide is just a moving float. To start with, try gliding toward the side of the pool or toward a friend.
1 Stand a couple of meters away from the side of the pool. With your arms outstretched, lean forward, bend your knees and
2 push off hard from the bottom of the pool. Straighten your legs and
3 let them rise to the surface. Keep your arms outstretched and your face in the water. Breathe out through partly closed lips. Your push should get you to the side of the pool.

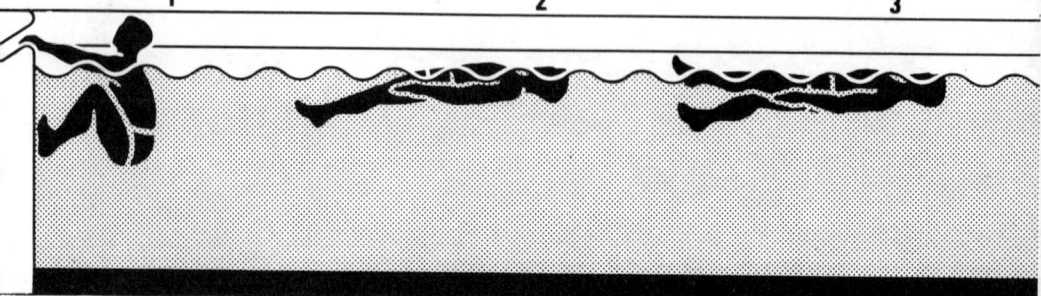

back glide (above)
1 Stand facing the side of the pool. Hold the rail with both hands, bring your knees up to your chest, and place your feet flat against the pool wall. Drop your head back and push off hard with your feet.
2 Straighten your legs, bring your arms down to your sides, and glide.
3 When you feel your glide is slowing down you can either stand up again, or keep yourself going by kicking your legs gently up and down, at the same time making a scooping motion with your hands. Once you have reached this stage you are all but swimming.

17

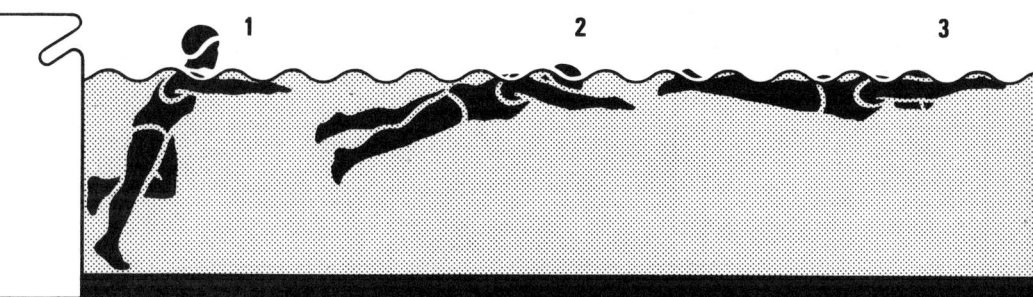

pushing off (above)
This time, instead of gliding toward the side of the pool, try gliding to the center.
1 Stand about shoulder-deep with your back against the pool wall. Bend one leg and place that foot flat against the wall. Stretch your arms forward, palms down. Lean forward and push off hard from the wall.

2 Breathe in deeply and lower your head between your arms, face in the water.
3 Keep your eyes open as you glide. Stand up when you run out of breath. If you have pushed sufficiently hard you should have traveled several meters.

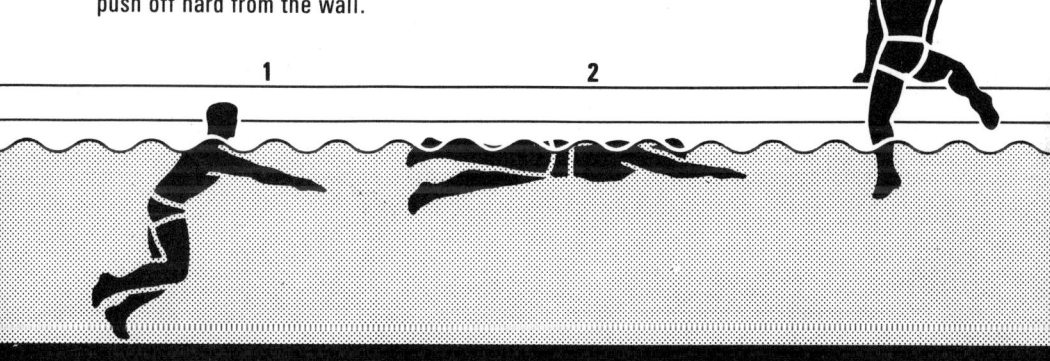

front kick (above)
1 Push off from the bottom of the pool, arms outstretched, and glide.
2 To keep moving, kick your legs alternately up and down. Keep your knees loose and relaxed and make sure that you kick from the hips. A good rhythmical movement is essential. Keep your arms outstretched, your face in the water, and your eyes open. Turn your head to one side when you need to breathe in.

getting out (above)
Basically there is only one way to get out of the pool without using the steps, and that is to clamber out. A good spring from the bottom will help you to get a grip on the side. Pull yourself up by your arms, throw one leg over the side, and clamber out.

Basic safety

It is never too early to get used to the water; even before you have mastered any of the strokes you can float in the water. But, right from the start, safety is an important factor. On this page we show different ways of treading water. Anybody can tread water and it is a good exercise to learn for two reasons: it helps you to develop a good strong leg kick, which is essential for all swimming strokes, and it is an important survival technique.

floats (above)
There are a variety of floats that you can use when you first start swimming—armbands, rubber rings, or the inner tube of a tire. They are all great fun to use but you should try not to rely too much on any of them; water itself will support you quite easily.

treading water (below)
In general, leg action is the most important aspect. There are a number of actions that you can use:
1 the scissors kick in which your legs open and close just like a pair of scissors;
2 the bicycling kick in which, as its name suggests, you move your legs as if you were riding a bicycle; and
3 a frog-like kick in which you circle your feet alternately backward, outward, forward, and backward again.
Arm action is not strictly a part of treading water, but
4 sculling with the hands can be used to supplement the kick. For this you rotate your wrists, palms outward and downward. For survival purposes it is essential you should be able to tread water with
5 one hand held above water, or
6 both hands above water.

Lakes, rivers and seas

Swimming in lakes, rivers, or the sea is very different from swimming in the confined space of a swimming pool. In one way it is much easier, because salt water is more buoyant than the water in a pool. But there are many more potential dangers—tides, currents, cold, and even various animals such as sharks or jellyfish. Swimmers and nonswimmers alike should take care not to get into difficulties. Even if you can swim, stay in shallow water and never swim by yourself.

heavy sea
Getting back to shore in heavy sea is not quite as daunting as it might seem. Basically you let the waves do the work for you:
1 swim toward the shore in the trough of a wave;
2 as a new wave comes up behind you, turn back to meet it;
3 swim through the wave and
4 ride it toward the shore.

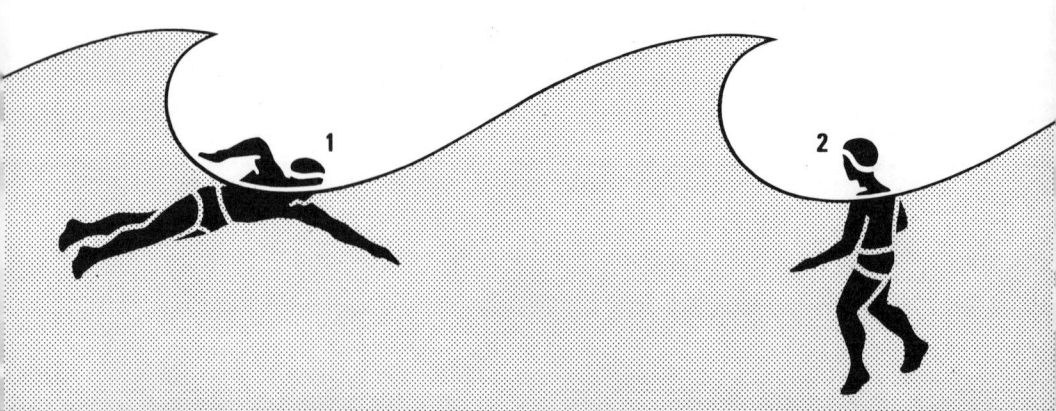

floating (below)
When you first get into the sea, stay in shallow water. Sit on the bottom, head above water. Lean back slightly and your legs will float up to the surface of their own accord. You can stay floating on your back, arms resting on the bottom, for as long as you like, just getting used to the feel of the water. To float on your front, kneel on the bottom on all fours. Again, let your legs float up to the surface, keeping your hands on the bottom. Once you have got used to the feel of the water you can work with a partner, practicing the floats and glides that you have learned in the swimming pool.

Dynamics

Swimming is not just a matter of floating on the surface. To be a good swimmer you have to be able to overcome water resistance; only then will you be able to swim fast and well.

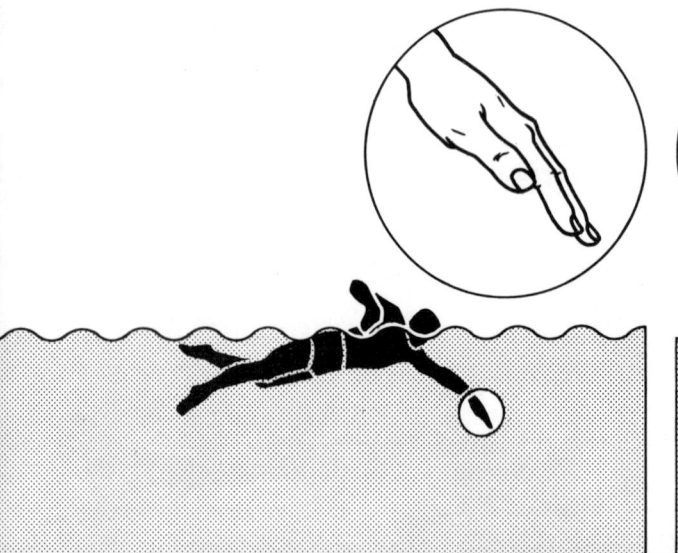

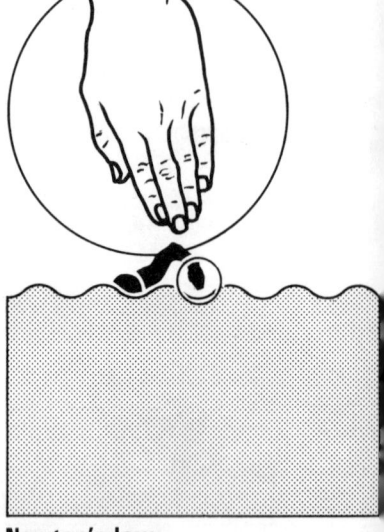

water resistance
Water resistance to a swimmer is caused in three ways—by the waves in front of him, by the friction of his skin and body hair, and by the whirlpool of molecules pulled forward by his body. To overcome water resistance a swimmer must be as streamlined as possible, rather like a speedboat. In the case of the crawl, this means lying flat, face-down on the water, wrists straight, hands flat, and fingers fairly close together to get the maximum pulling effect. The elbows should be bent and kept close to the body. Streamlined in this way the body is easier to propel with kick and arm stroke.

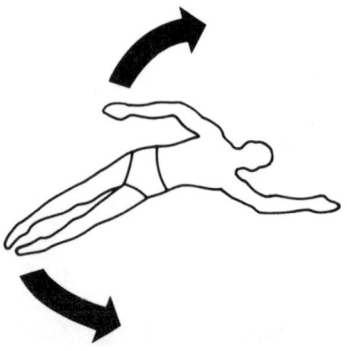

Newton's law
The dynamics of swimming essentially have to do with Newton's third law of motion. This states that every action results in an equal and opposite reaction. Translated into swimming this means that just as you press against the water so it presses against you.

recovery
Arm recovery above the surface is as important as the movement below. When the arm moves over the surface and forward an opposite reaction takes place in the hips and feet. In order to keep moving straight ahead rather than sideways, the elbow must be lifted and kept as close to the body as possible.

Most propulsion comes from a good, strong arm stroke. If the wrist is bent, the fingers are kept open, or the elbow makes too wide a sweep, power and propulsion are immediately lost. The hands must be kept straight and the fingers together. Similarly, if the head is kept up, the legs sink. Water resistance is greater and propulsion that much harder.

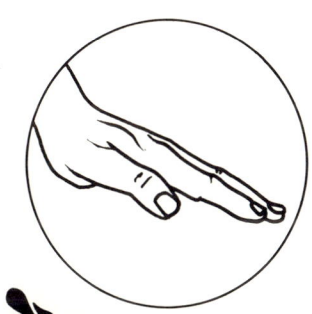
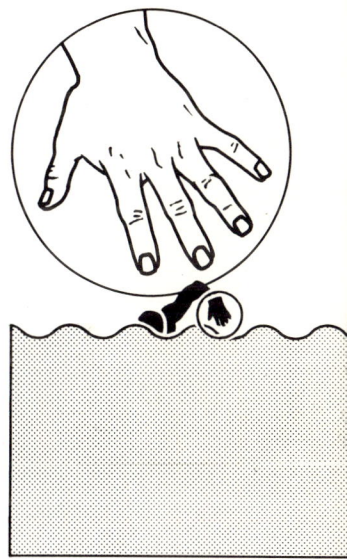

arm action

One smooth continuous movement is more effective than a series of jerky movements. For this reason the crawl with its continuous overarm action is faster than the breaststroke or butterfly. Your arm should act like an oar, entering the water parallel to your shoulder, pressing down, pulling through, and pushing back out of the water. It is this forceful, continuous movement that propels you forward.

Strokes

Strokes

In this chapter we show you how to do a variety of swimming strokes ranging from the dog paddle—the first stroke of all—to the strenuous but exhilarating butterfly dolphin. A knowledge of different strokes increases the enjoyment of swimming but in addition many of them are either vital for lifesaving or needed for skin-diving or water games.

The breaststroke was the first basic stroke to be taught. With the development of competitive swimming, other strokes such as the crawl were developed and refined for greater speed.

Dog paddle and trudgen

dog paddle (above)
The dog paddle may not look particularly elegant but it is the first true swimming stroke learned by most people and is quite a good jumping off point for the more sophisticated crawl. You can even start off with armbands or a flotation jacket.

1 Start in a float position, head out of water, elbows bent and close to your sides; keep your hands straight, fingers fairly close together;
2 reach with right hand; pull left hand toward your chest;
3 reach with left hand; pull right hand toward your chest. The legs should be kept almost straight, kicking alternately from the hips. Arms stay under water;
4 reach with right hand; pull left hand toward your chest;

trudgen (above)
Although now supplanted by the crawl, the trudgen is still a fast, reliable stroke. Essentially it is a sideways crawl made up of a scissors kick and a circular arm movement. The body lies flat on the water, twisting to one side for breathing purposes.

1 Start in a float position, right arm forward, left arm down by left thigh;
2 bring left arm out of the water and pull right arm back through the water; draw right leg up for scissors kick and press left leg back;
3 swing left arm around in a semicircle to the front of the head; roll to the right;
4 breathe in, and kick legs together.

5 reach with left hand; pull right hand toward your chest. The legs should be kicked alternately from the hips, keeping the knees bent. Arms stay under water the whole time, elbows kept close to the body. In effect you move your arms in much the same way as you would if you were hand-pedaling a bicycle.

Breathing presents no problem as the head is out of water all the time.

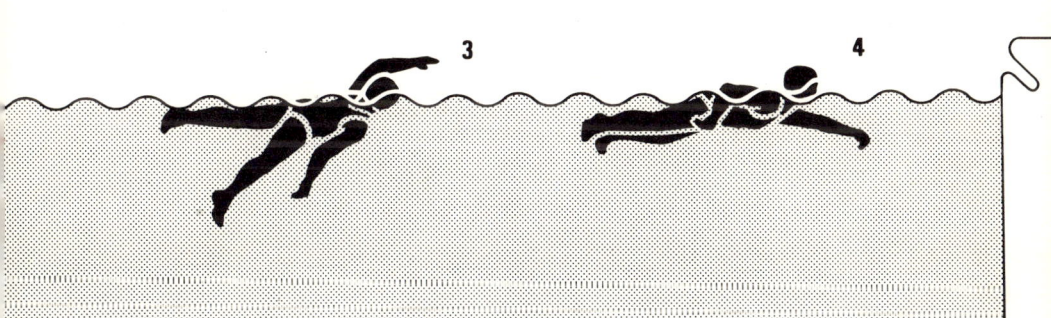

Side and backstroke

side stroke (below)
This is a very graceful stroke and one that has proved invaluable for long-distance swimming and lifesaving. As shown here the description applies to a person swimming on his left side; reverse the directions if you prefer to swim on your right.
1 Start with your legs together, right arm by your side, palm down, and left arm stretched forward; rest your head on your left shoulder, face turned to the right;
2 breathe in; pull your left arm toward your chest and bring your right arm up to meet it; move your right leg forward and your left leg back, keeping your knees slightly bent;
3 straighten your legs and bring them sharply together in a scissors kick; breathe out; at the same time sweep your right arm down and back to your thigh while sliding your left arm forward to its original position;
4 hold the glide or rest position for as long as possible before the next stroke.
Done correctly this stroke requires minimum effort. There should be no splashing because leg and arm action both take place under water.

Elementary backstroke (below)
Essentially this is an inverted breaststroke. It is easy to learn and is used a great deal in lifesaving, particularly for towing another person. Breathing presents no problem as the face is out of water the whole time. Lie horizontally in the water, legs straight, feet together, and arms by your sides, palms down;
1 bend your elbows and draw your hands up the

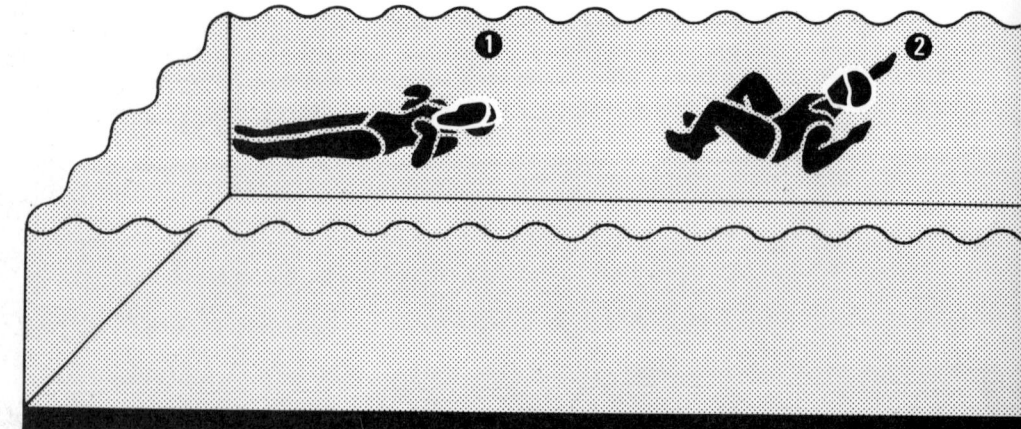

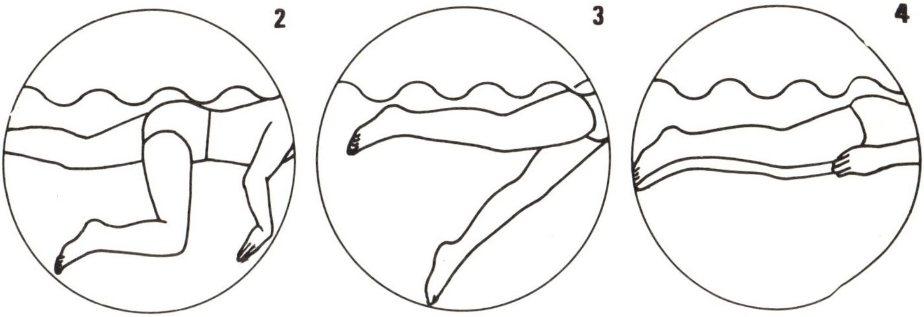

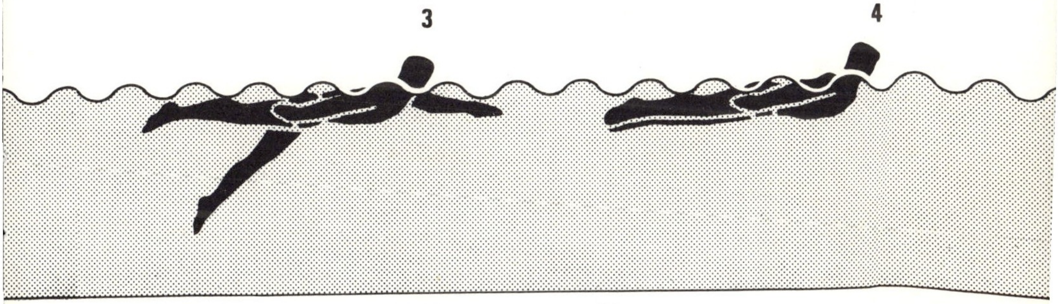

sides of your body toward your shoulders, turning your hands palms upward;
2 as your fingers reach your armpit, begin the leg recovery; draw your legs up under your body, heels together, knees spread;
3 drive your arms and legs out to the side,
4 pull your arms around in a semicircle back to your body, and complete the kick by sweeping your legs back together. Glide and repeat the stroke.

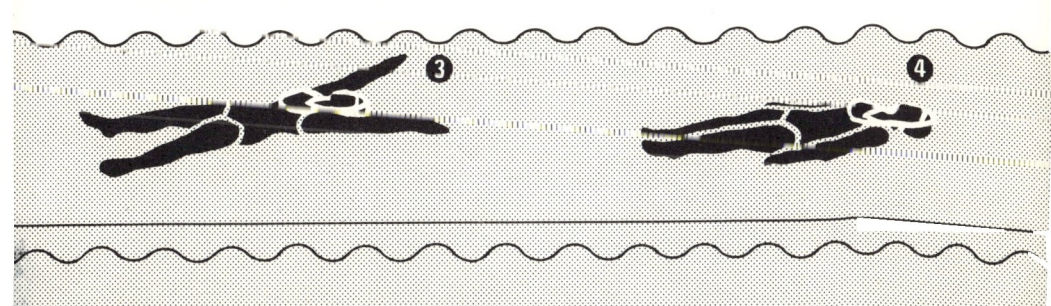

The crawl

The crawl is the fastest of all strokes—it should be as streamlined as possible with no twisting, rolling, or splashing. There are three basic aspects to the crawl that have to be combined— leg action, arm action, and breathing. These should be learned separately and then coordinated for the whole stroke.

practice with a partner (below)
The arm stroke is the driving action of the crawl. Basically each arm goes through an alternate cycle of reaching for the water, pressing down, and a fast over-surface recovery. Using a partner to guide your arms and an inflated ring for extra buoyancy, practice the cycle:
1 press your right arm slowly into the water as your left arm finishes its recovery;
2 press your left arm slowly into the water as your right arm begins recovery;
3 continue to press into the water with your left arm while speeding up recovery of the right arm;
4 as you finish pressing with your left arm, finish recovery of your right arm. Kick your legs while practicing; you will find that your arm and leg actions synchronize naturally.

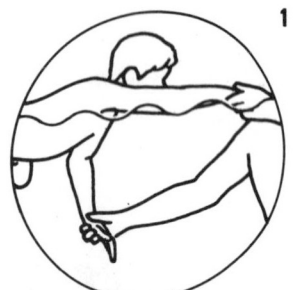

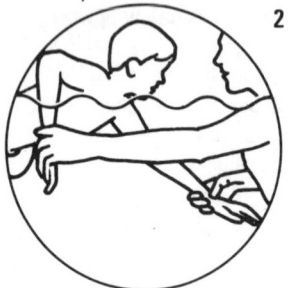

practice
1 Hold the rail with both hands; kick your legs up and down alternately from the hips. Keep your legs relaxed, knees slightly flexed. Aim for a steady, continuous movement. Avoid splashing; your legs should be under water all the time with only the heels breaking the surface; on the downward stroke let your feet go no more than nine inches below the surface.
2 Stand in shallow water leaning forward until your shoulders are submerged; start with your right arm down by your thigh, left arm forward, elbow slightly bent, and hand palm down just above the surface; press this arm down and back to your thigh; at the same time bend and lift your right arm out of the water and forward to the starting position. Most of the propulsion comes from the arm stroke so you should aim for an alternate reach-and-pull motion, one arm pulling as the other reaches out.

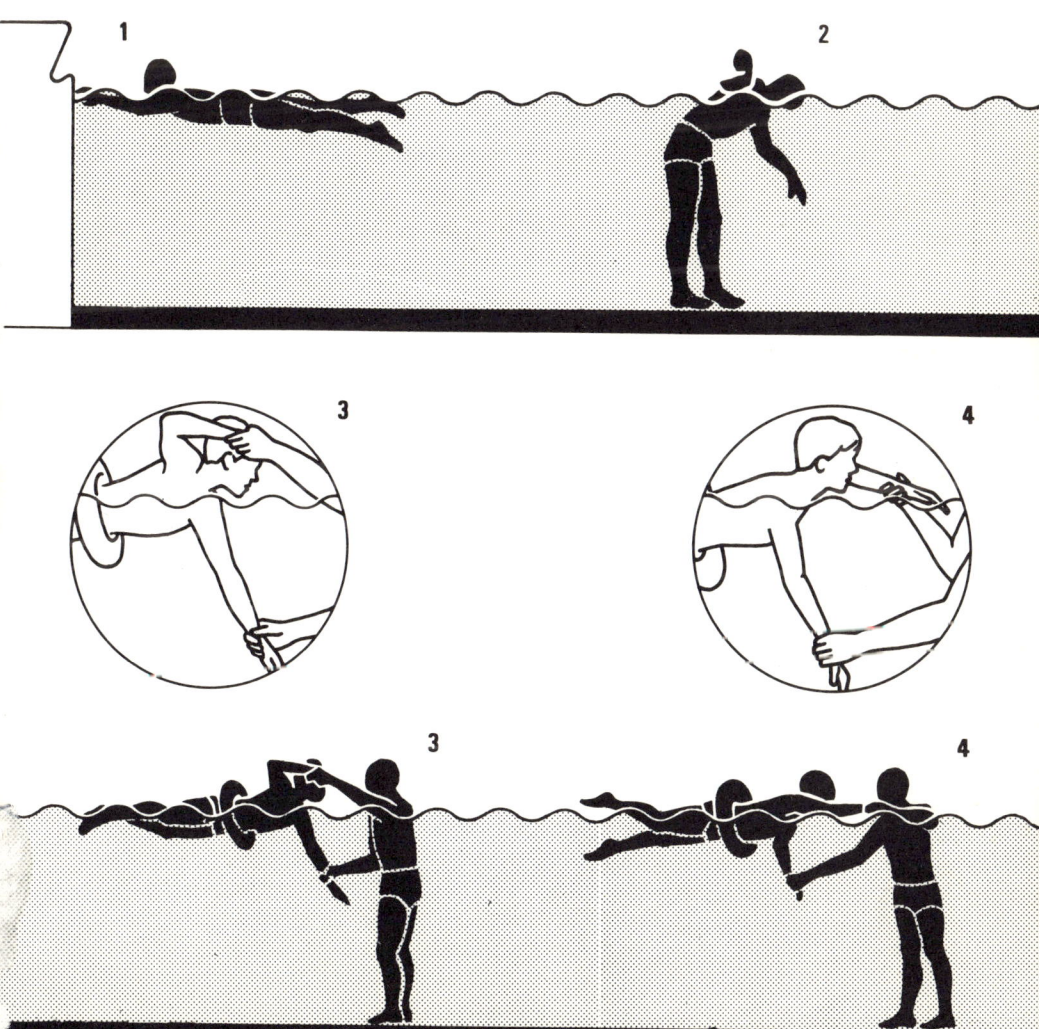

Front crawl

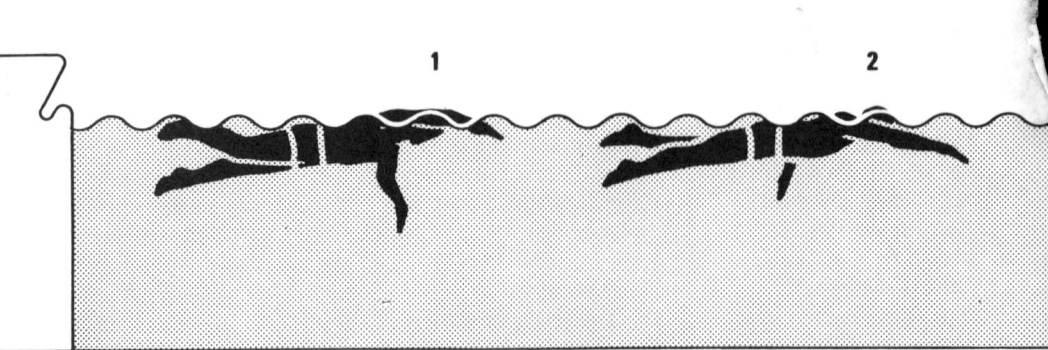

front crawl
As shown here the description applies to a person breathing to his right; reverse the directions if you prefer to breathe to your left.
1 press right arm forward into the water, hand flat, fingers fairly close together; pull left arm through
2 as far as thigh; press right arm down and back and
3 start bringing left arm out of the water elbow first; breathe out steadily;
4 bring left arm sharply out of the water; push back with right arm;
5 bring left elbow over the water in an arc, hand entering the water thumb first;
6 reach into the water with left arm;
7 bring right arm through as far as the thigh; start pulling left arm through the water;
8 bring right elbow out of the water; turn head to the right and breathe in;
9 pull through with left arm; recover right arm.

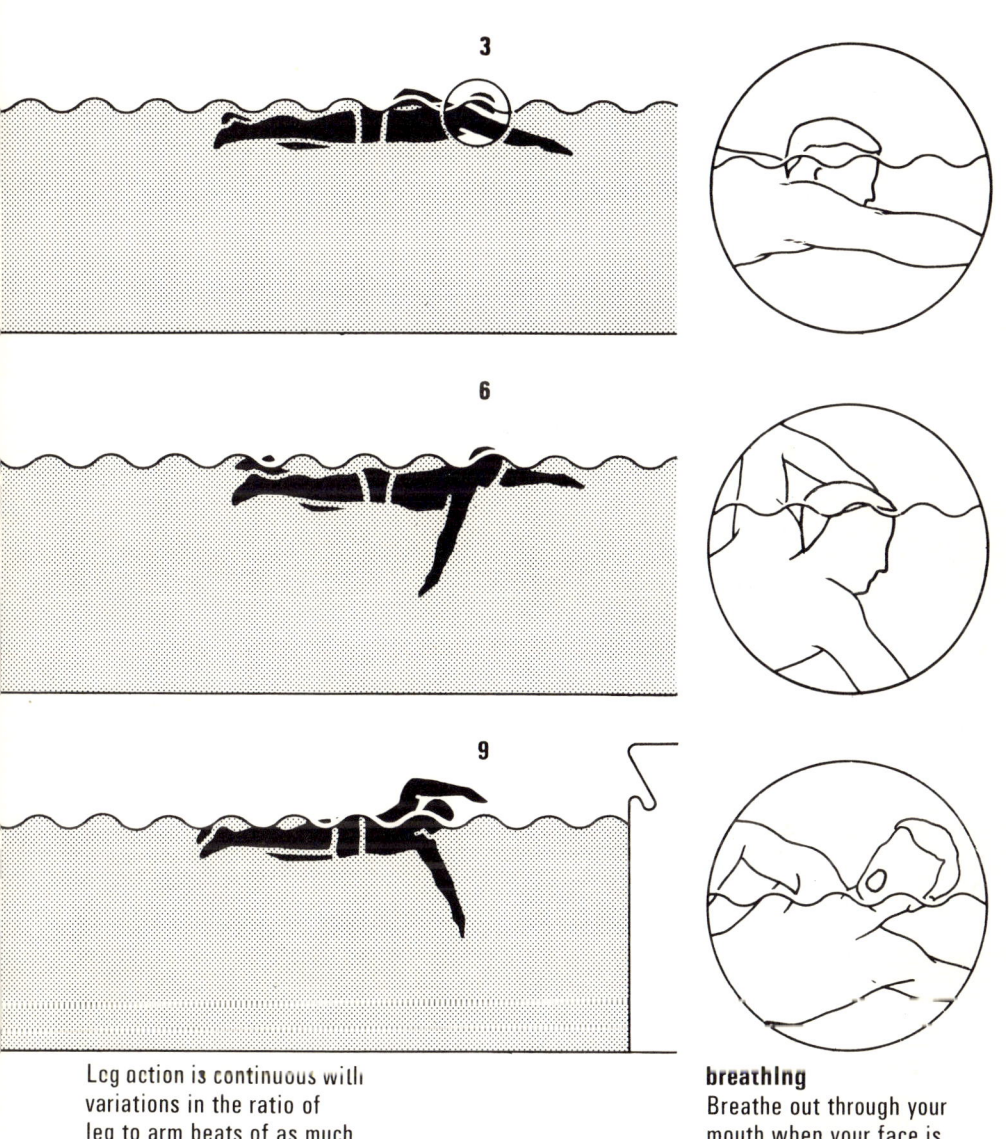

Leg action is continuous with variations in the ratio of leg to arm beats of as much as two, four, or six leg beats to every arm cycle—that is, one, two, or three leg beats to a single arm stroke.

breathing
Breathe out through your mouth when your face is submerged and while the left arm is recovering; breathe in through the mouth by turning your head to one side while the right arm is recovering.

Breaststroke

The breaststroke is one of the most restful ways of moving through the water. Unlike the crawl, the arms move simultaneously, as do the legs. Both movements should be perfectly symmetrical. They can be practiced separately in the water, or the whole stroke can be practiced at home, lying on the floor or over a chair.

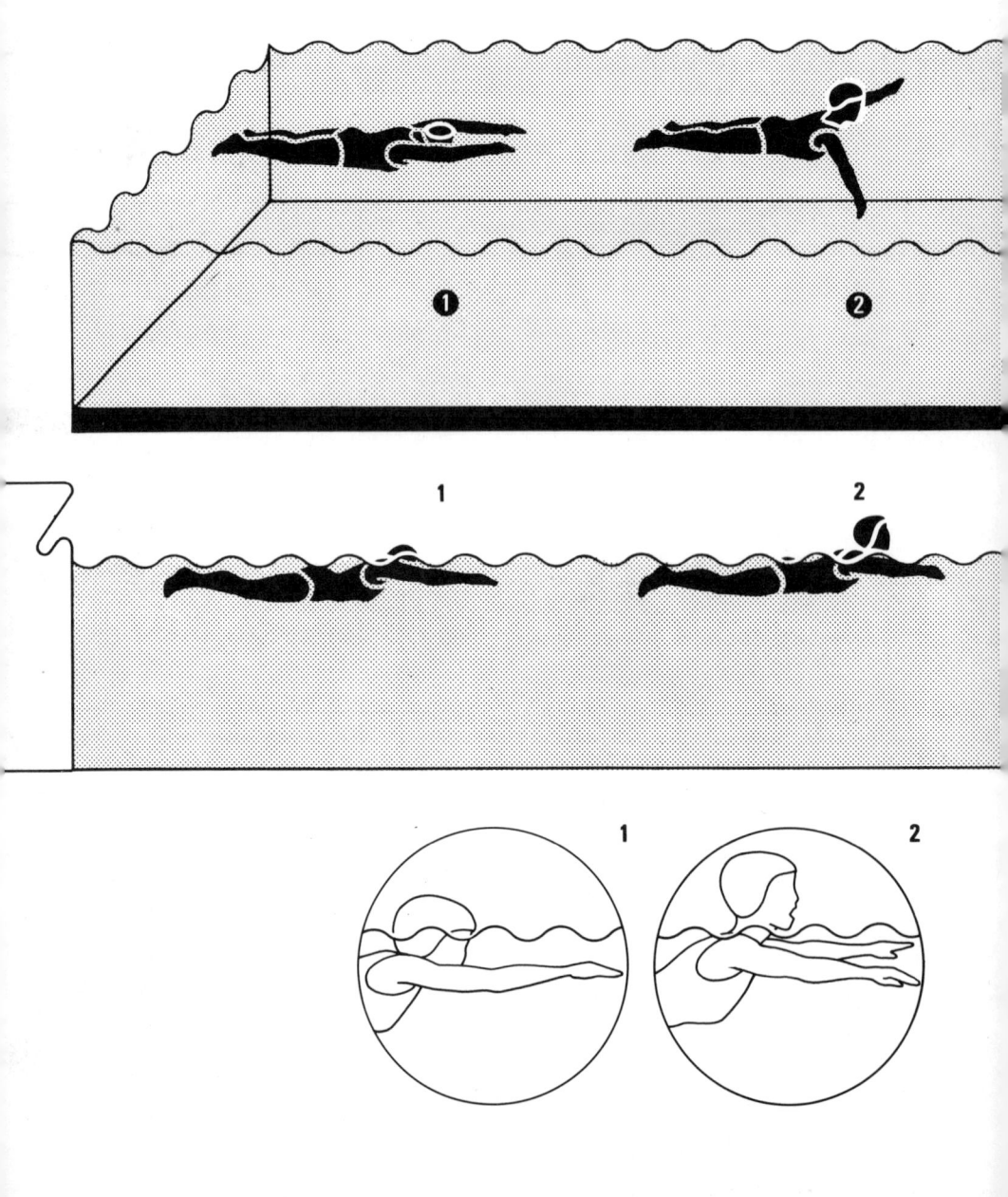

breaststroke

1 Glide face down, arms and legs straight, hands and feet together;
2 move your arms apart in the beginnings of a circular movement; lift your head and breathe in;
3 bend your elbows, bringing your hands up, palms downward, in front of your chin; at the same time bring your knees forward and outward, with your heels together;
4 whip your legs out and backward, shoot your arms forward and
5 bring your legs sharply together; glide and breathe out into the water.

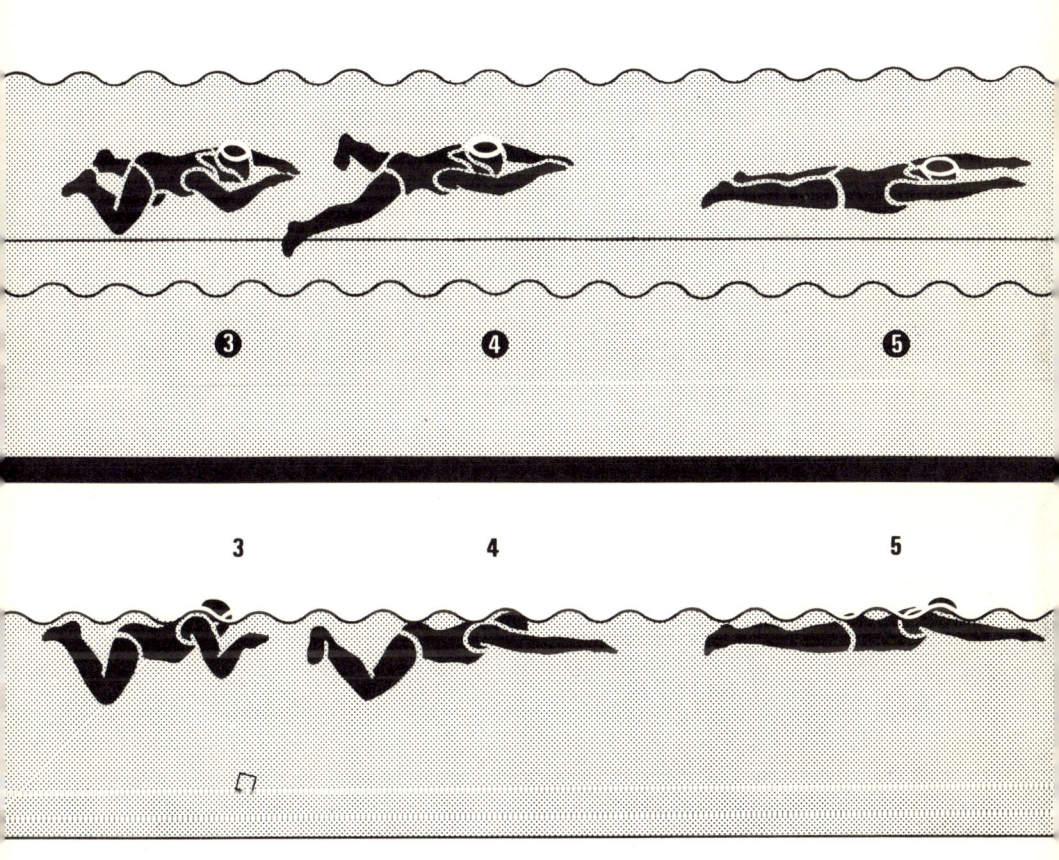

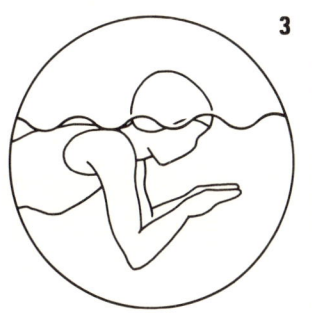

breathing

Breathing is closely linked to the action of the arms and head. Start the stroke with head down, arms stretched out, hands together, thumbs touching, palms down and slightly cupped. As you move your arms to the side and then back under your chest, your body will be lifted up. This is when you should raise your head and breathe in. You should lower your face and breathe out as your arms are brought forward again.

Back crawl

The back crawl is exactly as its name suggests—a crawl swum on the back. In one way it is easier to learn, as the face is out of water and breathing is almost natural. The kick is much the same, with the legs moving up and down as if kicking off a pair of shoes. The arm action is a continuous circling movement. The hand enters the water straightened, fingers fairly close together pulling downward like the oar of a boat and forward against the water. The arms are always directly opposite each other.

back crawl
1 Left arm enters the water above the shoulder, palm outward; right arm presses down past the thigh;
2 bring right arm out of the water, palm downward, pull left arm sideways through the water and press down
3 to the thigh as right arm reaches high point of arc;
4 press right hand down as left arm finishes recovery;
5 push left arm past thigh as right arm slices water, palm outward;
6 push right arm sideways through the water; sweep left arm above the water;
7 push right arm toward thigh as left arm reaches high point of arc;
8 bring right arm through the water, palm downward, for recovery; bring left arm down toward the water. The power pull starts as the hand enters the water. If the swimmer were lying on a clock face the right hand would enter the water between 10 and 11 o'clock and the left hand between 1 and 2 o'clock. The arm should be straight, palm vertical, so that the little finger enters first.

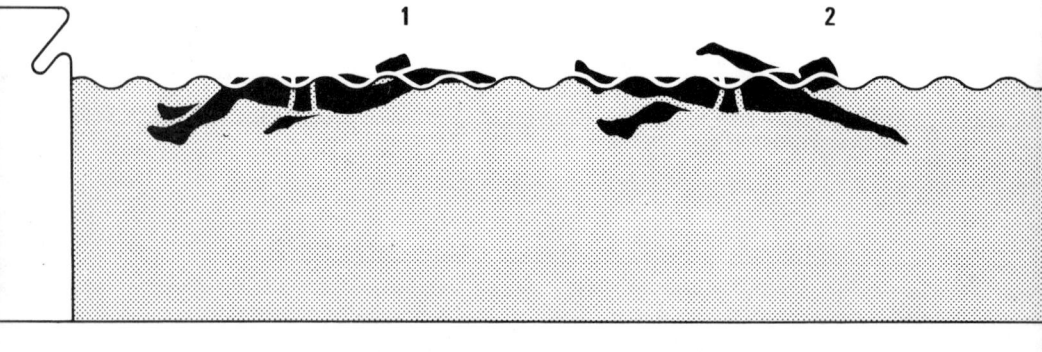

3   4

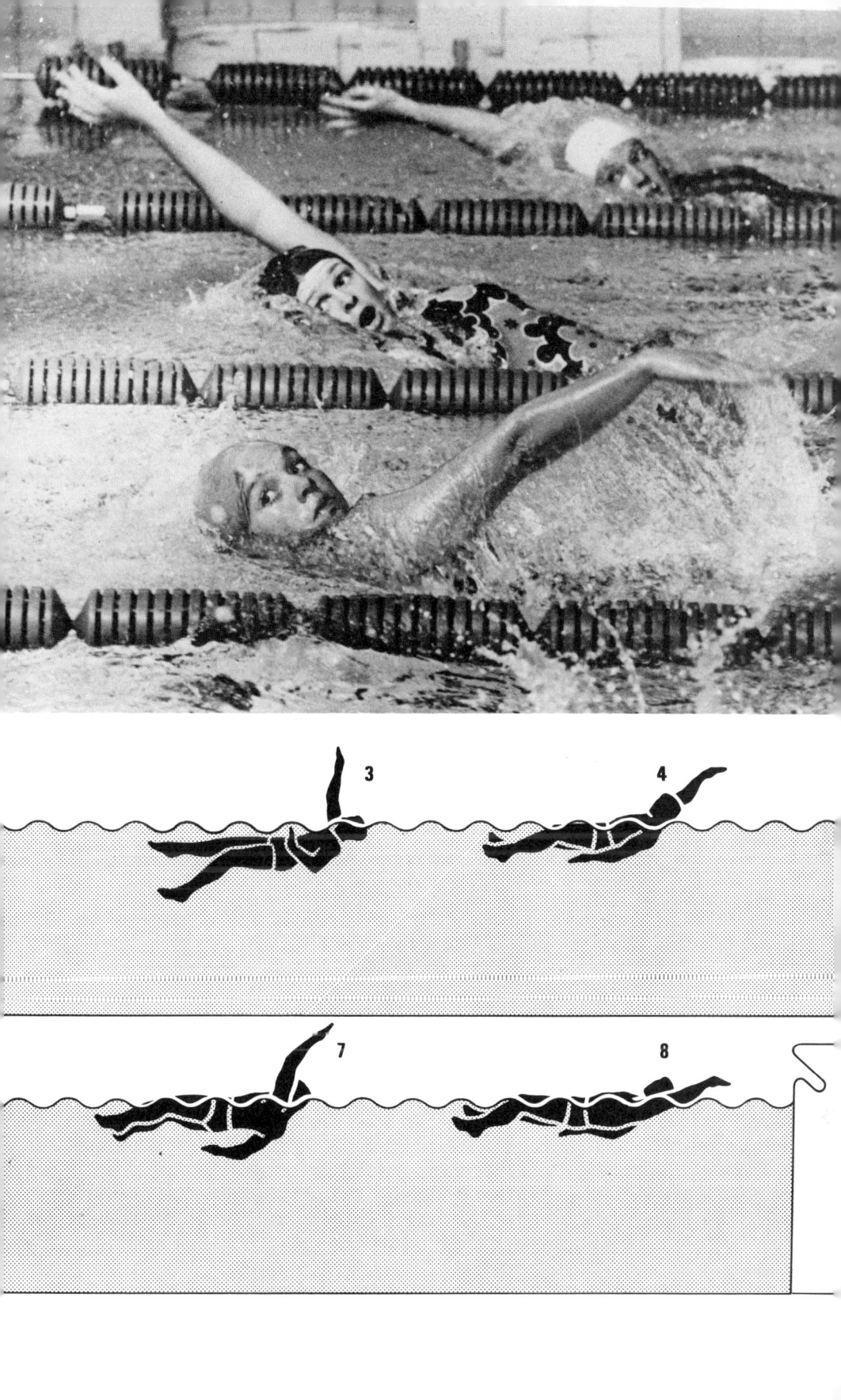

7   8

Butterfly dolphin

Although there is little similarity today, the butterfly dolphin began as a variation on the breaststroke. It was created in the 1930s and was finally recognized in 1953. It is a difficult and complicated stroke to master and can be exhausting. The legs move together in an up-and-down wave-like motion similar to a dolphin's tail. The arms, which recover low above the water, work together and resemble the beating wings of a butterfly. There are two leg beats to one arm stroke.

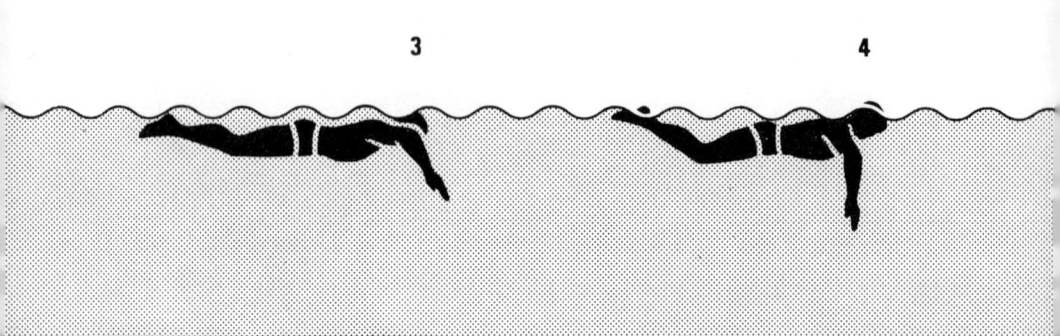

butterfly dolphin
1 Arms enter water in line with shoulder; feet kick downward;
2 feet are straightened in line with body; hips rise to surface;
3 hands are pressed in an outward and downward direction with elbows bent and kept high;
4 hands come nearly together under chest;
5 legs complete downbeat then;
6 arms leave water and legs are brought upward without bending;
7 arms are recovered over the water; head is lowered, feet almost break surface at start of second kick;
8 swimmer exhales at start of arm pull;
9 arms finish pull, second kick is made and breath is taken;
10 the arms are recovered over the water and head is lowered face down.

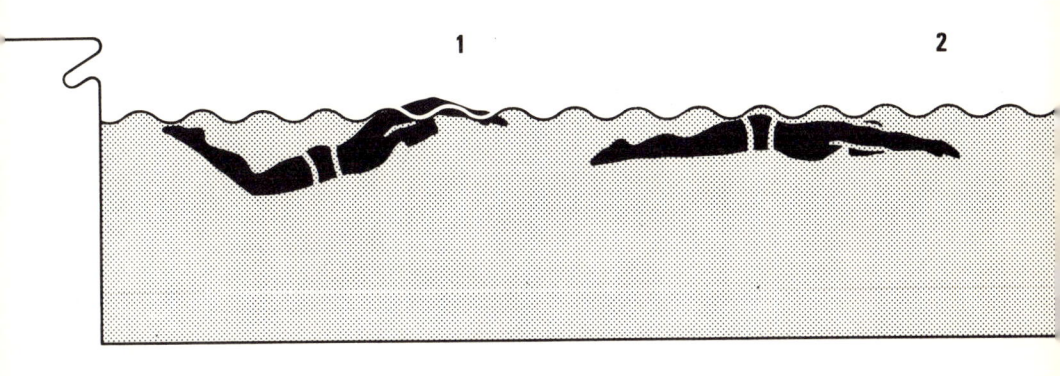

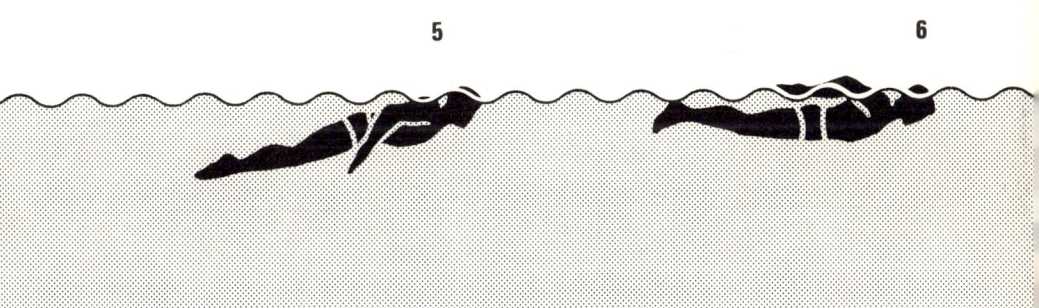

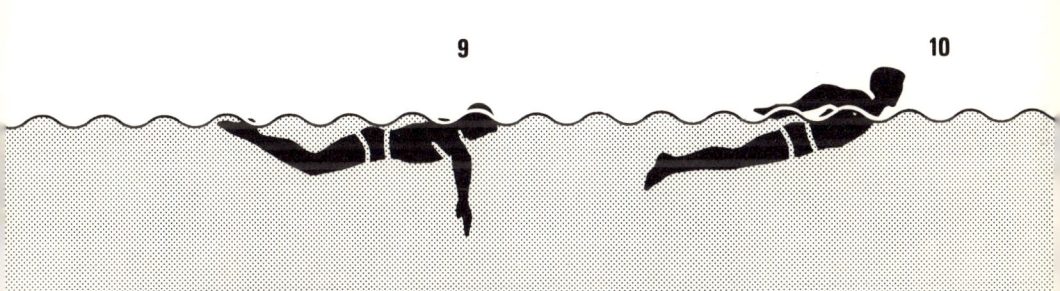

It is the leg movement that gives the stroke its speed — the butterfly dolphin is second only to the crawl. Basically the kick is similar to that of the crawl; movement begins at the hips but both legs work in unison to produce a wave-like motion.

Breathing can be done in two ways. In the first the head is turned to one side as in the crawl. In the second the head is kept forward and lifted as the arms begin to leave the water. Whichever method is used breathing always takes place at the end of the arm pull and the second downbeat of the legs.

Competition swimming

No one knows where or when the first swimming competition was held. Certainly swimming was an important activity in Ancient Greece and Rome where it was mainly used in the training of soldiers. Although swimming declined in the Western world, it remained popular in Japan where, in 36 BC, some of the first recorded swimming competitions took place. In 1603 it was again in Japan that inter-school swimming contests were ordered by Imperial edict.

Modern competitive swimming began in Britain in the 19th century. The oldest acknowledged national swimming body was formed in London in 1869. It later became known as the Amateur Swimming Association and laid down rules of competition. Other countries followed suit and by 1908 a world-governing body, the Fédération Internationale de Natation Amateur (FINA) was formed. The federation laid down international rules and created an official world record list. These rules applied to the Olympic swimming events, which had been open to men from 1896 and to women from 1912. Today swimming is the second most important event in the Olympic Games.

British swimmers dominated the early Olympic events but were superceded by the United States, who continue to dominate these events today.

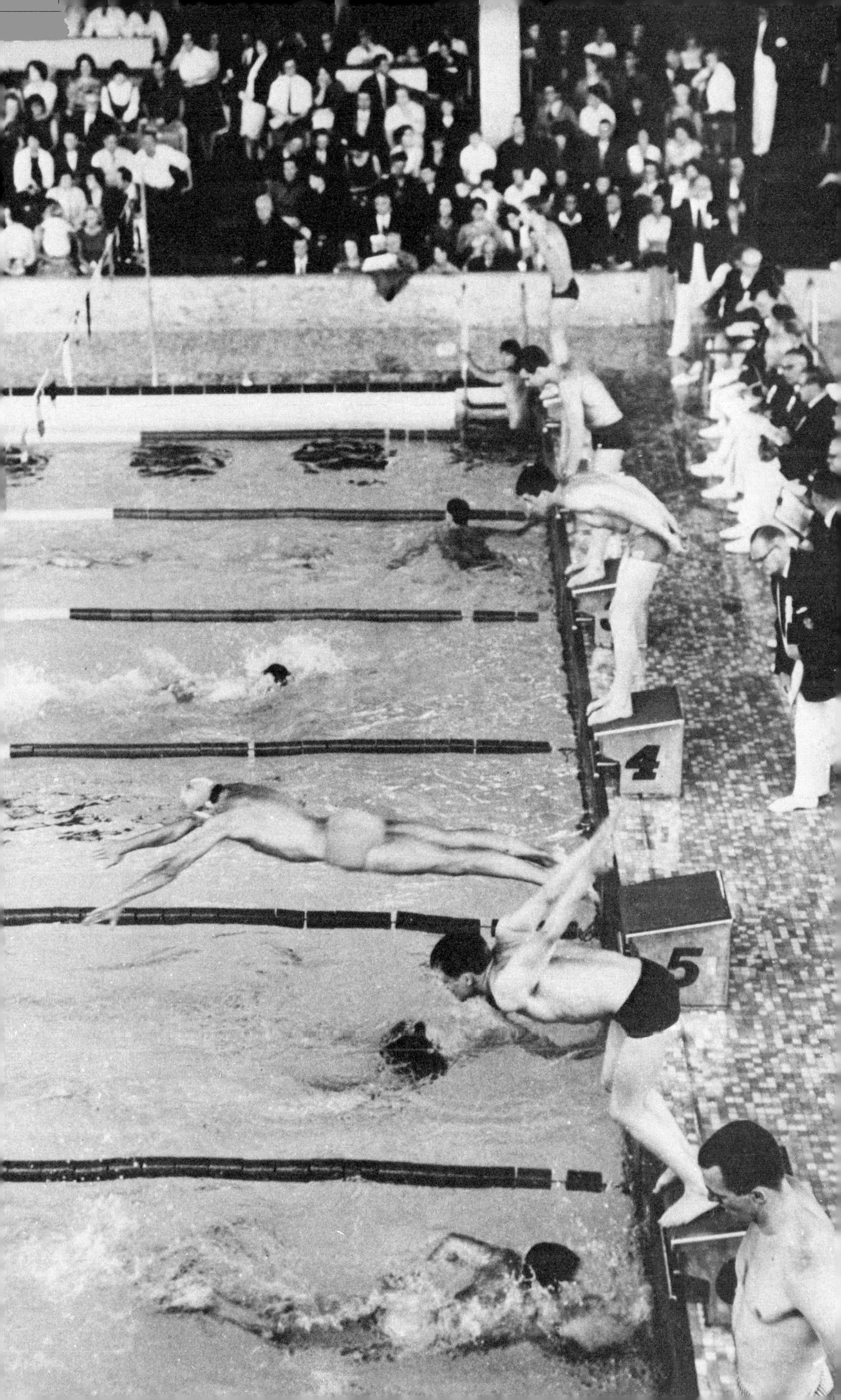

4
5

Rules

Swimming is both an individual and a team water sport. Participants compete in races and the first swimmer to cover a predetermined distance is the winner. Competitions are held in four major categories of swimming stroke: freestyle, breaststroke, butterfly, and backstroke.

the pool
Competitions are held in pools of varying lengths, but in the Olympic Games, a 50m (54.7yd) pool is used. The pool is divided into eight lanes, numbered one to eight from right to left. Each swimmer must remain in his own lane.
In all events except the backstroke, swimmers ideally start with a dive from starting blocks.

dress
Men must wear swimming trunks, and ladies a one-piece costume with shoulder straps extending from front to back. All swimwear must be nontransparent. Caps are optional.

officials
Minimum international requirements are a referee, a starter, a chief timekeeper, three timekeepers per lane, a chief judge, three finishing judges per lane, one inspector of turns per lane at both ends, two judges of strokes, one recorder, one clerk of course, plus additional timekeepers to replace those whose watches did not start.

the referee (a)
The referee has overall control, ensuring that the rules are obeyed, inspecting the course, and adjudicating in any disagreements between officials or competitors.

the starter (b)
The starter controls the competitors until the race has begun. He must ensure that each swimmer is in his correct lane, and he and the referee are the only judges of whether the start is valid.

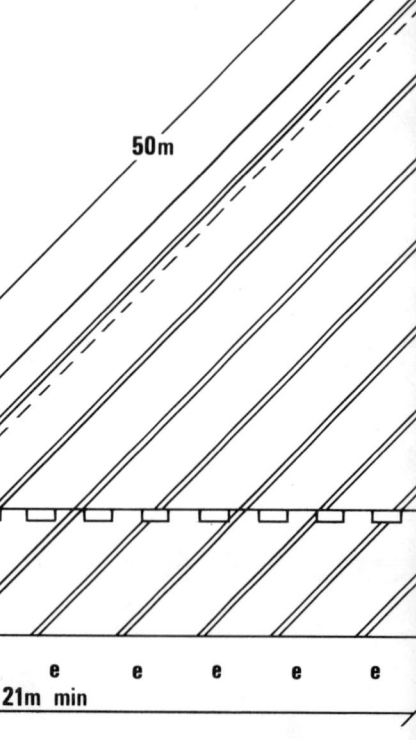

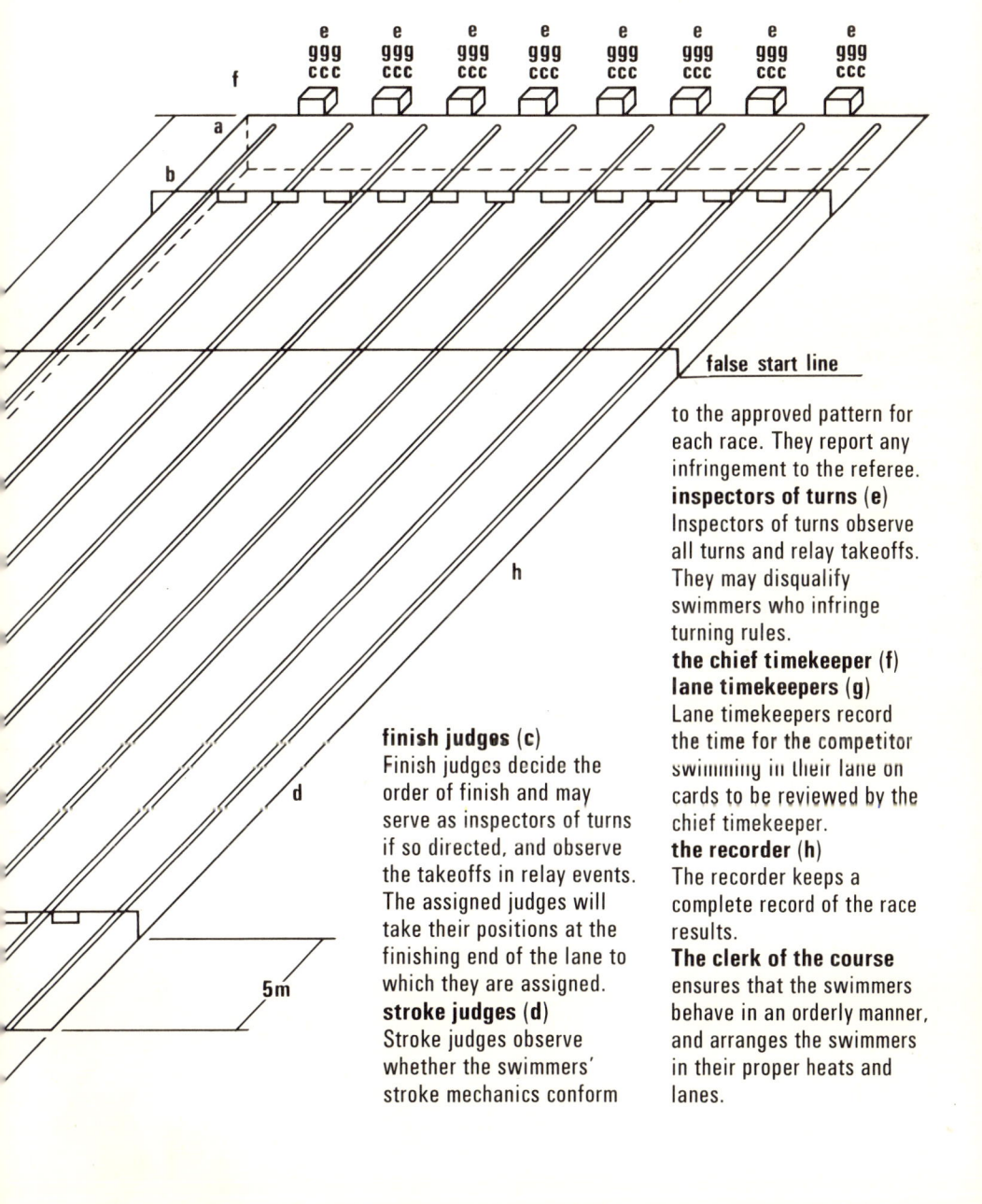

false start line

to the approved pattern for each race. They report any infringement to the referee.

inspectors of turns (e)
Inspectors of turns observe all turns and relay takeoffs. They may disqualify swimmers who infringe turning rules.

the chief timekeeper (f)
lane timekeepers (g)
Lane timekeepers record the time for the competitor swimming in their lane on cards to be reviewed by the chief timekeeper.

the recorder (h)
The recorder keeps a complete record of the race results.

The clerk of the course
ensures that the swimmers behave in an orderly manner, and arranges the swimmers in their proper heats and lanes.

finish judges (c)
Finish judges decide the order of finish and may serve as inspectors of turns if so directed, and observe the takeoffs in relay events. The assigned judges will take their positions at the finishing end of the lane to which they are assigned.

stroke judges (d)
Stroke judges observe whether the swimmers' stroke mechanics conform

Rules

the start

Except in the backstroke, the competitors step up to the back of the starting blocks at the referee's call. Then, on the starter's command "Take your marks," they immediately step forward to the front of the blocks and assume a starting position. Only when they are all quite stationary will the starter give the signal for the race to begin. The starting signal may be a shot or an electronically activated horn.

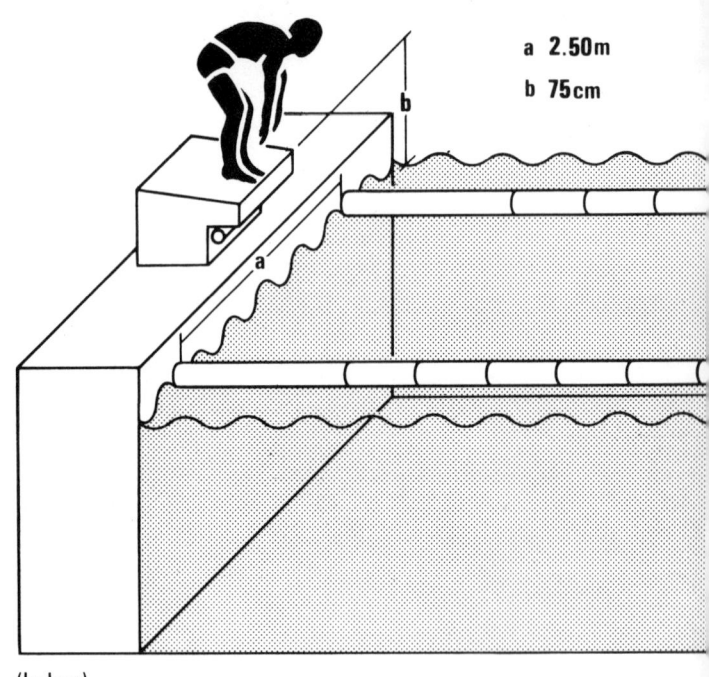

a 2.50m
b 75cm

(below) starting position for forward strokes

the spearhead principle
In each event the competitor with the fastest entry time is assigned the center lane, or—in pools with an even number of lanes—the lane on the right of the center. The other swimmers are placed alternately left and right of him in descending order of speed, so that the slowest swimmers are in the two outside lanes.
If the entry times are a true indication of form, the swimmers will fan out into a spearhead formation during the race.

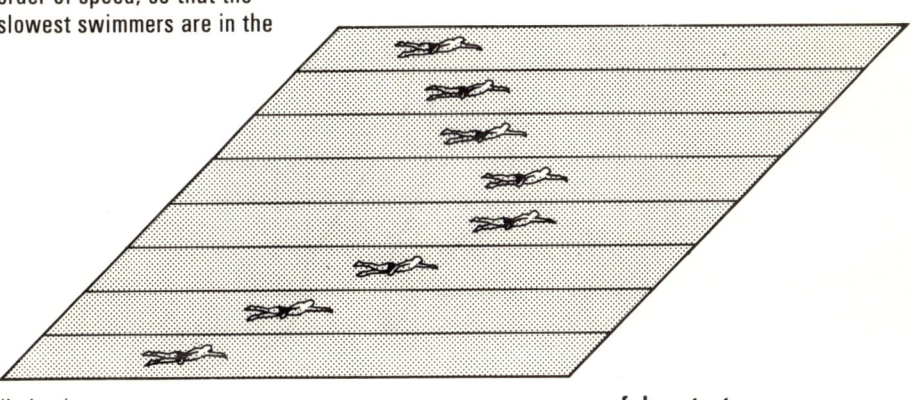

(below)
starting position for backstroke

false start
The starter recalls the competitors at the first or second false start, but at the third attempt to start the race, a swimmer who breaks before the starting signal is given is disqualified and the race proceeds.
The swimmers are recalled after a false start by the lowering of a rope onto the water.

Rules

freestyle
Freestyle swimming means that in an event so designated the competitor may swim any style; but in a medley relay or individual medley event, freestyle means any stroke other than back, breast, or butterfly stroke.
In freestyle turning and finishing the swimmer can touch the wall with any part of his body. A hand touch is not obligatory.
The stroke generally chosen is the front crawl.

front crawl
The main characteristics of this stroke are the following: each arm is alternately brought over and then into the water, while the legs perform a kicking action. The swimmer generally breathes on one side in the trough made by the arm pull.

backstroke
The competitors line up in the water, facing the starting end, with the hands placed on the starting grips. The feet, including the toes, must be under the surface of the water. Standing in or on the gutter, or bending the toes over the lip of the gutter, is prohibited.
At the signal for starting and when turning, the swimmers push off and swim on their backs throughout the race. The hands must not be released before the starting signal has been given.

Any competitor leaving his normal position on the back before his head, foremost hand, or arm has touched the end of the course, for the purpose of turning or finishing, shall be disqualified.

clarification of turn
It is permissible to turn over beyond the vertical after the foremost part of the body has touched, for the purpose of executing the turn, but the swimmer must have returned past the vertical to a position on his back before the feet have left the wall.

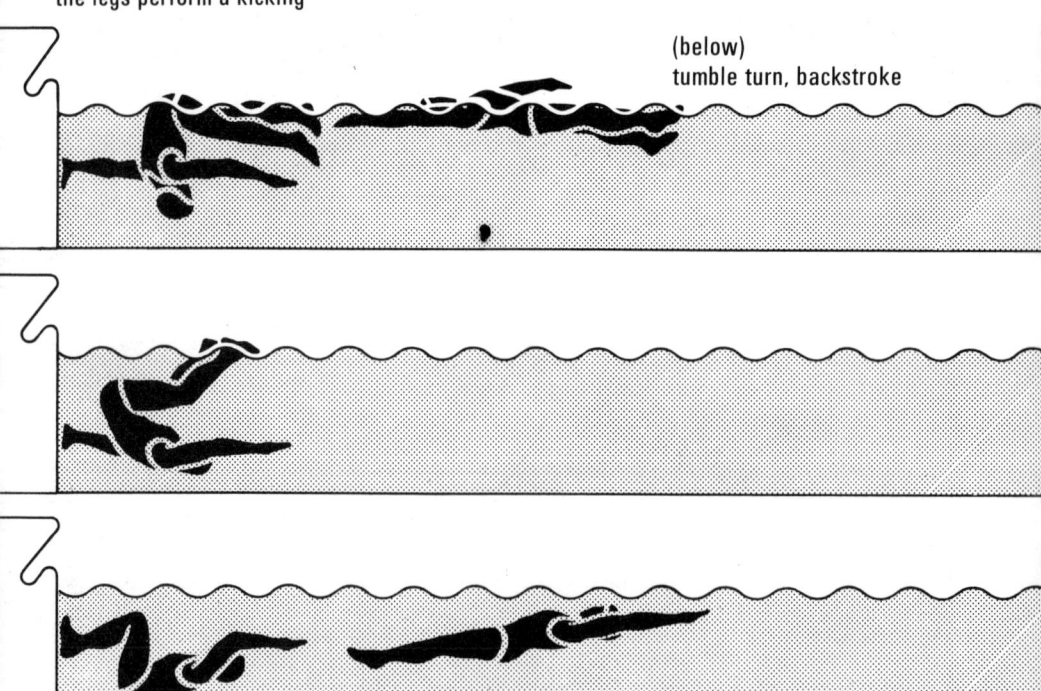

(below)
tumble turn, backstroke

(below)
tumble turn, front crawl

Rules and events

butterfly stroke
Both arms must be brought forward together over the water and brought backward simultaneously. The body must be kept perfectly on the breast and both shoulders in line with the surface of the water from the beginning of the first arm stroke, after the start and on the turn.
All movements of the feet must be executed in a simultaneous manner. Simultaneous up-and-down movements of the legs and feet in the vertical plane are permitted. The legs or feet need not be at the same level, but no alternating movement is permitted. When touching at the turn or on finishing a race, the touch must be made with both hands simultaneously at the same level, and with the shoulders in the horizontal position. The touch may be made at, above, or below the water level.
At the start and at turns, a swimmer is permitted one or more leg kicks and one arm pull under the water, which must bring him to the surface.

breaststroke
The body must be kept perfectly on the breast and both shoulders must be in line with the water surface from the beginning of the first arm stroke after the start and on the turn.
All movements of the legs and arms must be simultaneous and in the same horizontal plane without alternating movement. The hands are to be pushed forward together from the breast, and brought back on or under the surface of the water. In the leg kick the feet must be turned outward in the backward movement. A "dolphin" kick is not permitted.
At the turn and on finishing the race, the touch must be made with both hands simultaneously at the same level, either at, above, or below the water level. The shoulders are to be in the horizontal position.
Part of the head must always be above the general water level except at the

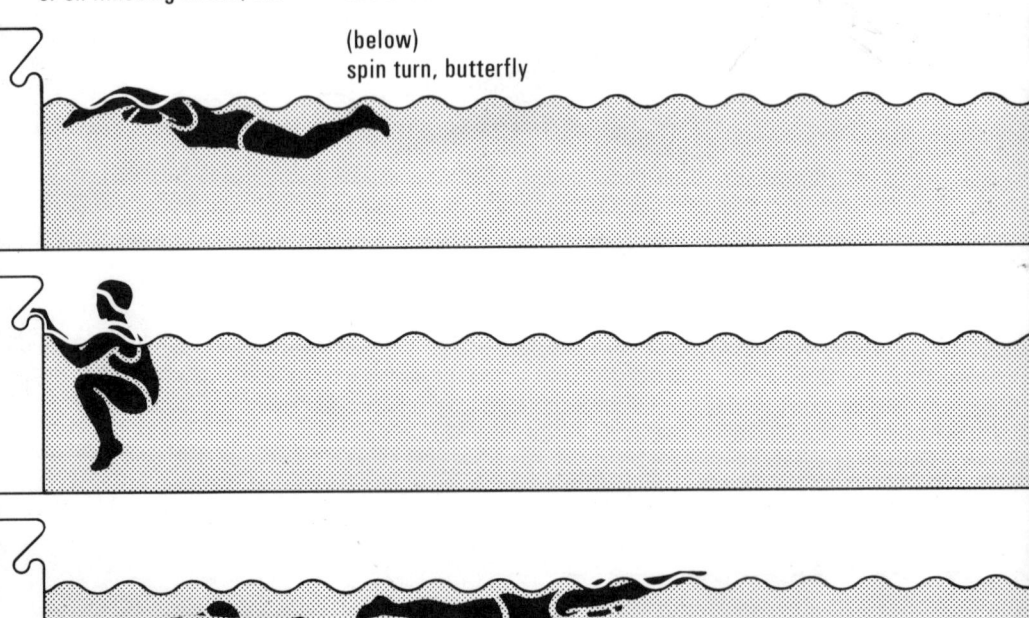

(below)
spin turn, butterfly

start, and at each turn the swimmer may take one arm stroke and one leg kick while wholly submerged before returning to the surface.

medley events
In individual events, competitors swim an equal distance of four strokes: the sequence is butterfly, backstroke, breaststroke, and freestyle. In medley relays, each swimmer swims one stroke for the set distance; the order is backstroke, breaststroke, butterfly, and freestyle.

disqualification
A competitor will be disqualified for: obstructing the progress of another swimmer; swimming out of lane (except that he is allowed to submerge below the surface in order to return to his proper lane); walking (though not standing) on the bottom of the pool; leaving the starting block in a relay race before his preceding partner touches the wall (unless he returns to the wall in default); not finishing the whole course if swimming alone; wearing or using any device to aid speed, buoyancy, or endurance (such as webbed gloves, flippers, fins, etc.); not making physical contact with the wall at a turn or at the end of a race (it is not permitted to take a stride or step from the bottom of the bath); entering the water while a race is in progress, or entering a race for which he is not listed.

Olympic events (for both sexes):
100m freestyle
200m freestyle
400m freestyle
800m freestyle
1500m freestyle
100m breaststroke and butterfly stroke
200m breaststroke and butterfly stroke
100m backstroke
200m backstroke
200m and 400m individual medley
4x100m freestyle relay
4x200m freestyle relay

(below)
spin turn, breaststroke

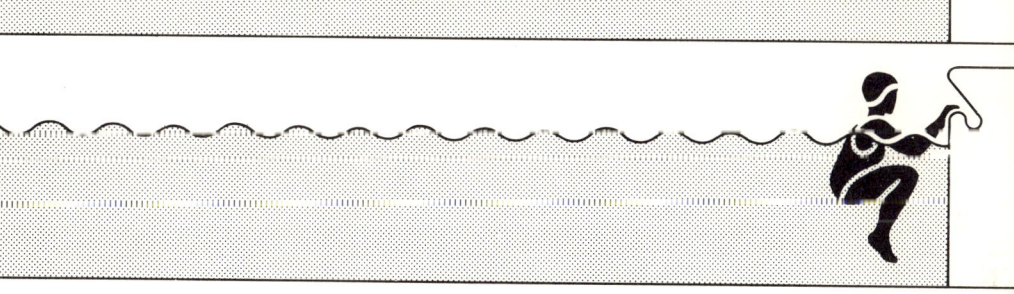

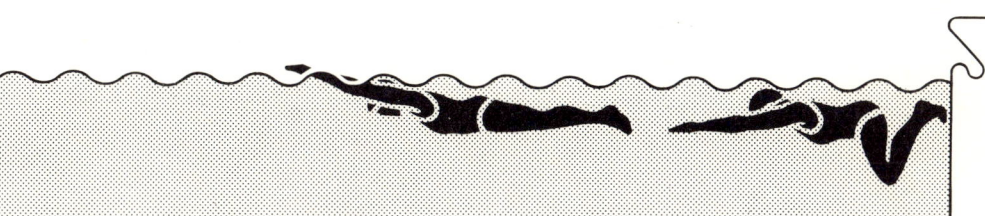

Diving

53

Diving

Diving is a thrilling pastime—it is one of the few sports where you can actually fly through the air without support. To start with, it takes a bit of courage to enter the water headfirst, but it is a wonderful feeling to be able to fly through the air and glide safely into the waiting water.

Although diving is a water sport, water only provides a landing area; the real skill takes place on the board and in the air. Whether it is a plain header or a complex aerial somersault, every dive requires perfect timing and absolute bodily coordination.

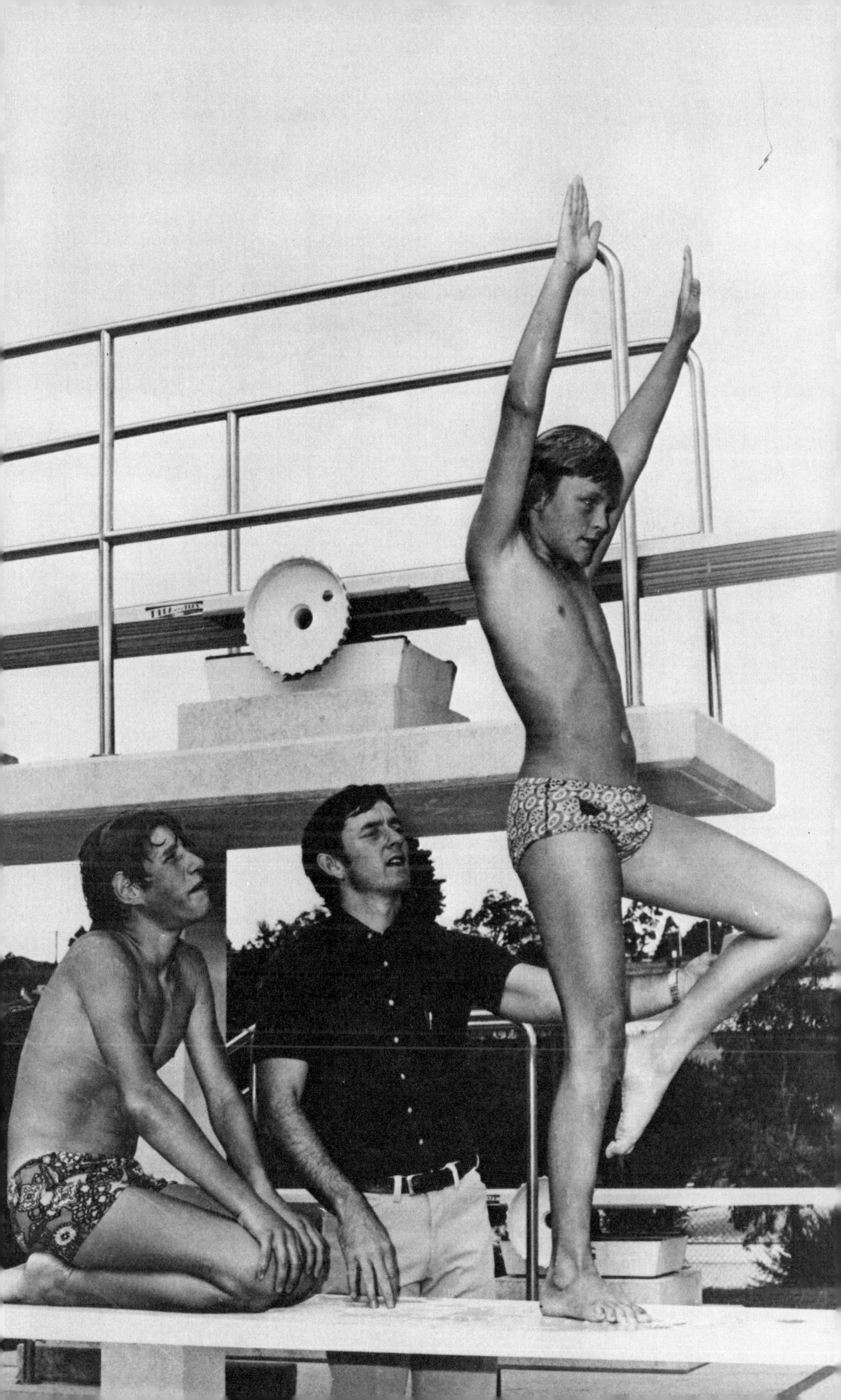

Getting started

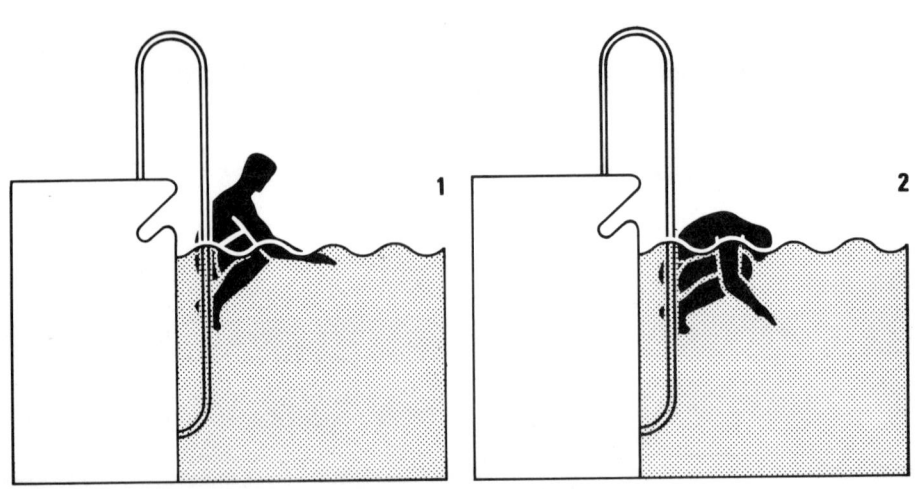

getting started (above) Learning to dive takes time and patience. Good diving needs confidence and it is best to learn in slow, easy stages. Remember that you should never do a standing dive from the side into less than 3m (10ft) of water. The simplest start is with a forward tumble into the pool from the steps or ladder.
1 Sit on the steps as close to the water as possible.
2 Bend down toward the water, head down and chin tucked well into your chest.
3 From this position roll into the water.
4 Push off and glide. Practice this entry several times to get used to the feel of putting your head under water, before moving on to poolside dives.

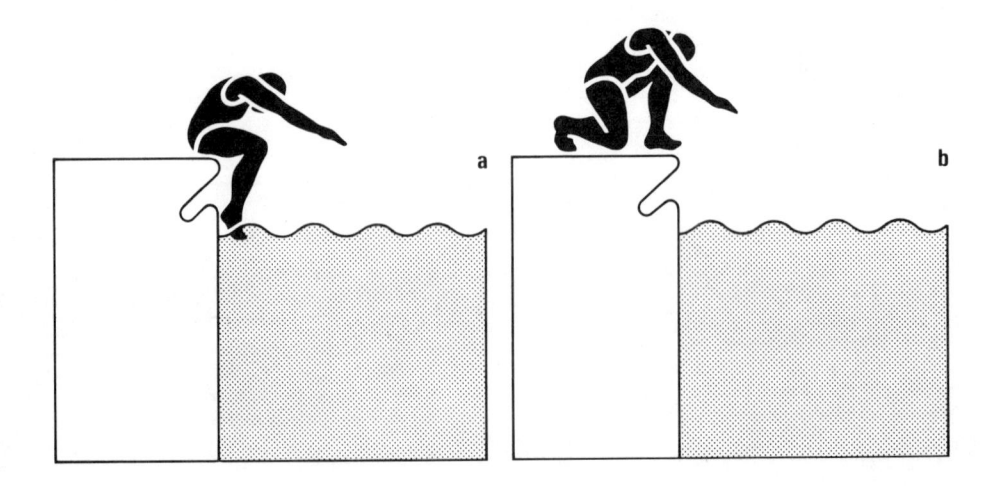

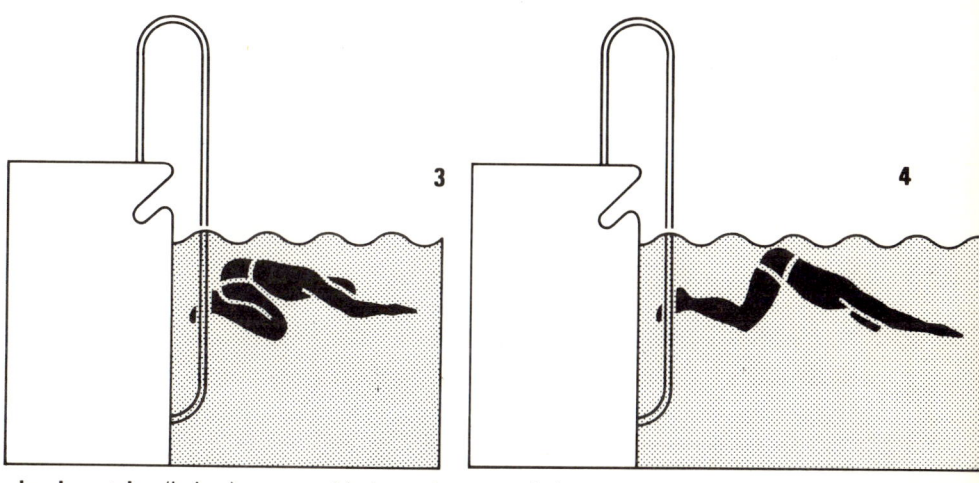

simple entries (below)
Practice headfirst entries stage by stage:
a Sit on the edge of the pool, feet in the water. Keep your head down, chin touching your chest. Roll in.
b Kneel on one knee. Stretch your arms forward and down. Keep your chin well down and push off.
c Stand one one leg with the other raised. Aim for the bottom, keeping your hands and head down. To start with, let an instructor help you by holding your rear leg and aiming you correctly. Kick your rear leg high to make a headfirst entry.
d Keeping your arms and head well down, take off from both feet, raising your legs and hips as in a handstand.

Basic dives

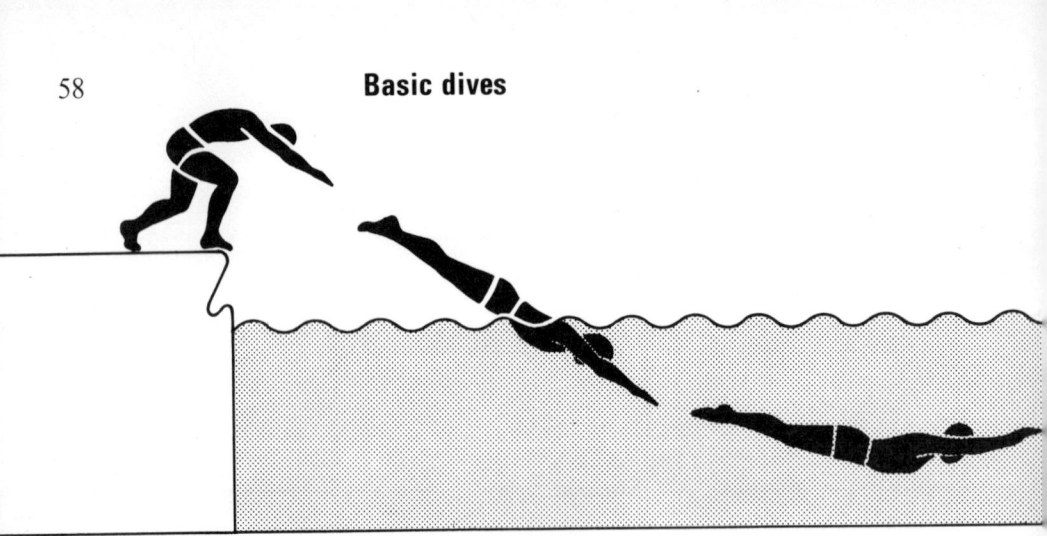

basic plunge (above)
Stand at the edge with your knees bent, one foot back, toes of the other curled over the edge. Stretch your arms forward and plunge into the water. Keep your head well down.

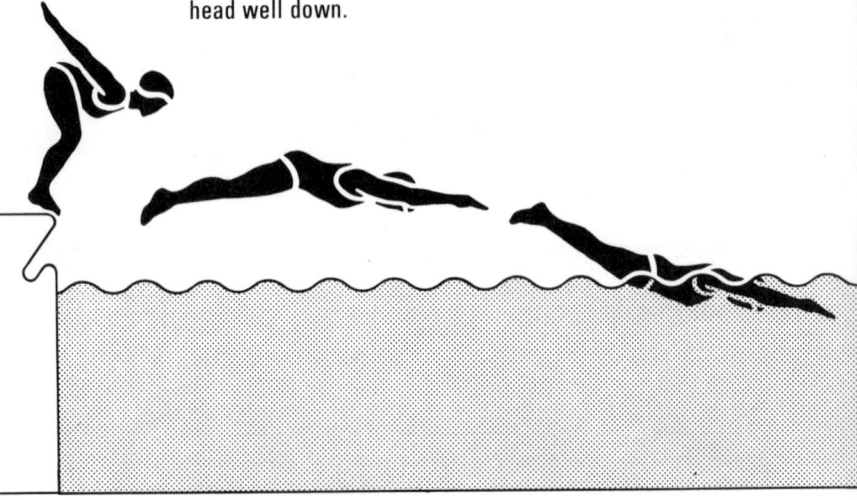

racing dive (above)
Stand with knees bent, arms back and head up. Swinging your arms down and forward, push hard out over the water. Drop your head forward. Enter the water at a shallow angle so that you glide for some distance just below the surface. As you surface, breathe and go into a fast forward stroke.

59

Board diving

Diving boards have come a long way from the shaky wooden highboards and rudimentary plank-like springboards that existed before the Second World War. Today highboards must be rigid and covered with a resilient hardwood surface. Springboards are made either of light aluminum alloy or of a thin wooden core surrounded by glass-fiber. Springiness varies from board to board but most have an adjustable fulcrum so that they can be altered to suit an individual diver or dive. Heights, widths, and lengths vary. Usually a pool has springboards of 1m (3ft 3in) and 3m (9ft 9in) high, and highboards ranging from 3m (9ft 9in) to 10m (33ft). The most important factor is the depth of water around the boards. For safety there should be 3m (10ft) of water not only below the entry spot but stretching 3m (10ft) in front, 1m (3ft 3in) behind, and 2.5m (8ft) to either side of the board.

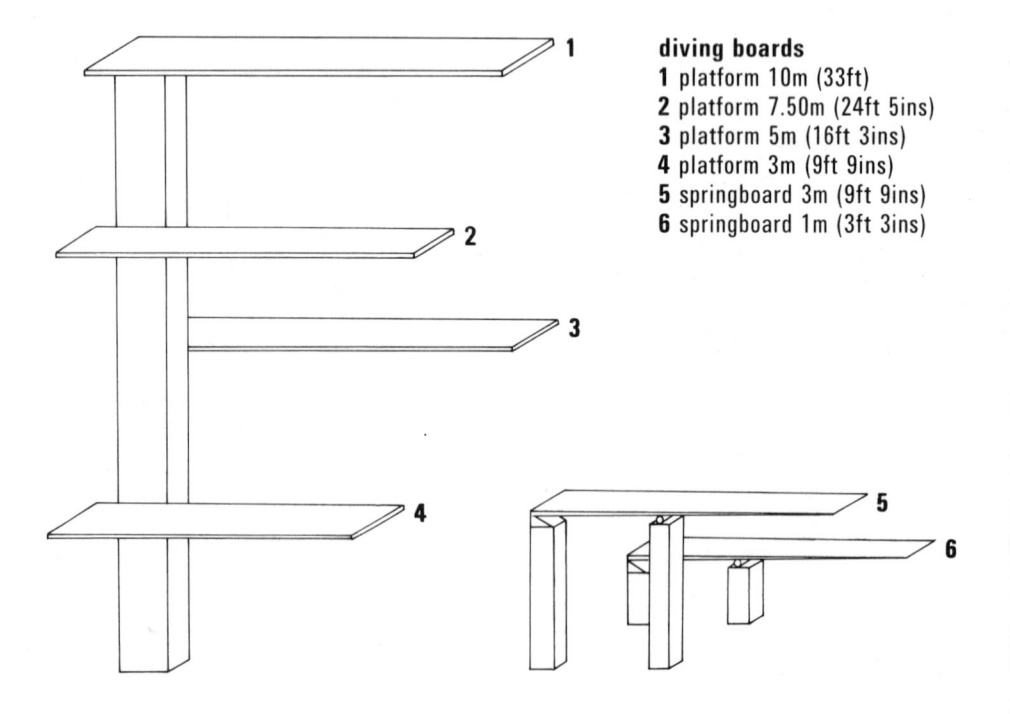

diving boards
1 platform 10m (33ft)
2 platform 7.50m (24ft 5ins)
3 platform 5m (16ft 3ins)
4 platform 3m (9ft 9ins)
5 springboard 3m (9ft 9ins)
6 springboard 1m (3ft 3ins)

takeoff
All dives take off from one of three positions—backward, forward, or from an armstand. Forward dives can be made either standing or running. Reverse dives take off facing forward but the body turns in the air. Inward dives take off backwards so that the diver enters the water facing away from the board.

positions
In the air there are three basic diving positions—piked, tucked, or straight. The piked position is also known as the jackknife. Essentially the body is bent at the hips but the knees are straight. In the tucked position the body is rolled into a ball with the hips and knees bent. In the straight or layout position, the body must be fully stretched without being bent at either hips or knees.

entry
A dive may finish headfirst or feetfirst but the body must always be vertical or nearly vertical when it enters the water. In a headfirst entry the arms should be stretched above the head, in line with the body. For a feetfirst entry the arms must be kept absolutely straight and close to the body.

Posture and exercises

Diving is a beautiful sport. It demands absolute coordination of the head, arms, knees, and ankles, and perfect balance. The exercises on this page are designed to achieve the sort of body control that turns a dive from a series of separate actions into one graceful, streamlined movement.

posture (above)
Imagine that you have a book balanced on your head. Stand erect but not stiffly, keep your stomach in and practice walking as smoothly as possible. Try and avoid unnecessary movements of the arms and hands.

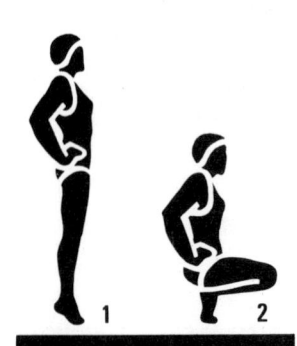

ankle exercise (above)
Do this exercise on land to develop a well coordinated ankle and knee action.
1 Rise onto your toes and drop back onto your heels.
2 Bend your knees so that they work with your ankles.

board exercise (above)
This exercise is designed to match the movement of the board:
1 rise on your toes lifting your arms and straightening your ankles simultaneously;
2 as the board rises slightly, sweep your arms up, rising on your ankles so that you bounce into the air.

standing front jump
(below)
This sequence will help you coordinate your movements with the natural springiness of the board so that you learn to get the proper lift on every dive:
1 stand erect, feet together, toes gripping the end of the board, arms extended for balance;
2 lower your arms, being careful to keep your balance;
3 sweep your arms up and forward, straightening your ankles at the same time to rise up on the balls of your feet;
4 bring your arms back and down, bending your knees and flexing your ankles until your heels are back on the board. Bring your arms back up again and, as the board is driven downward,
5 jump off, pushing hard with your legs and feet. In the air,
6 bring your arms down to a cross position and when you hit the water
7 close your arms to your sides and enter the water in an absolutely vertical position.

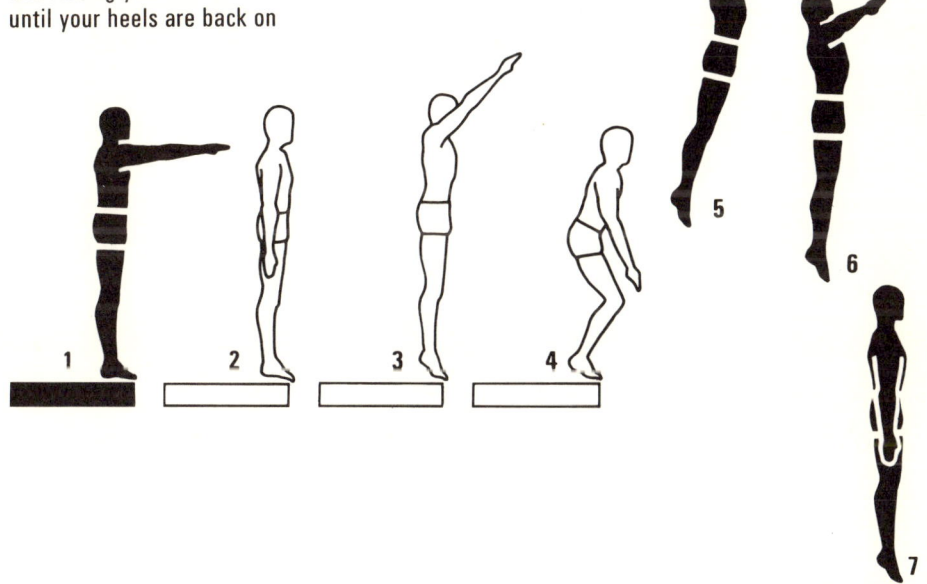

The approach

A good approach is the keynote to a perfect takeoff. Basically it consists of three or four steps and a jump, or hurdle, to the end of the board. It is an essential part of any running dive and should be practiced until you are certain of arriving at the end of the board absolutely balanced and coordinated.

the approach
1 stand erect, head up, arms relaxed;
2 begin walking forward on the left foot;
3 lengthen stride onto right foot, moving naturally from heel to toe;
4 lengthen stride again onto left foot;
5 move onto the right foot, bringing your arms slightly back;
6 bring your arms forward and lift your left knee high. Push down on the board with your right leg and
7 swing your arms forward and up springing up from the board, feet and toes pointed;
8 bring your legs together, arms out to the side, and drop back to the board;
9 bring your arms down as you land on the board, bend your knees, and push down hard;
10 continue to push and bring your arms up for takeoff.

65

front header
Push off from the board, arms stretched over your head, legs straight, toes pointed, and stomach muscles pulled well in. Keep your body straight and as you start to drop lower your head, entering the water as near vertical as possible.

The hurdle

It takes a lot of practice to achieve a well-balanced, well-timed hurdle but it is the most important part of board work. Basically it is a spring rather than a jump. You need to incorporate the movement of the board itself so that when you land back on the end of the board you get the greatest possible lift for your takeoff into the air.

hurdle positions (above)
There are three main types of hurdle:
a the broad jump hurdle, which is performed as a low long arc;
b the spot hurdle, which is a short hurdle. This does not make full use of the board's natural springiness, which means that a diver has to exert more pressure for takeoff;
c the high jump hurdle, which is the most effective of the three. It makes maximum use of the board, throwing the diver into a high arc from which he can perform the most complex dives.

cross position (above)
Once you have reached the highest point of your hurdle, straighten your legs and bring your arms into this horizontal cross position. This will balance you in the same way as a tightrope walker balances himself on the wire.

swan dive (below)
Drive up from the board, bringing your arms only slightly forward. Spread your arms out horizontally, holding this position as you reach the top of the dive. As you drop down, bring your arms forward and enter the water vertically.

forward pike (above)
Drive off from the board sweeping your arms above your head. As you approach the top of the dive, drive your hips up and bend sharply at the hips to form what is virtually a triangle. Touch your toes with your fingertips, keeping your legs and arms straight. As you descend straighten out and enter the water vertically, legs together, toes pointed.

back takeoff (above)
A successful takeoff relies on absolute coordination between the arms and legs.
1 stand at the edge of the board resting only on the toes and balls of your feet; keep your arms outstretched for balance;
2 lower your arms;
3 sweep your arms upward;
4 bend your knees and bring your arms into the cross position;
5 sweep your arms back ready for takeoff.

Back dives

A back dive can be frightening to start with; it is not natural to go through the air backward and upside down. Work with an instructor until you have enough confidence to try on your own. In a back dive you start from the end of the board with your back to the water—obviously an approach and hurdle are impossible—and continue backward through the air. If you dive from a 1m (3ft 3in) board to start with, even if you land flat on your back, no harm can come to you.

turning on the board (above)
Placing your weight on the ball of one foot, spin around so that your heels are at the end of the board.

back dive (above)
As the board drops drive up and backward, straightening your knees and ankles. Sweep your arms up and back into the cross position, arching your body at the top of the dive. Stretch out and reach for the water.

practice (above)
Let an instructor hold you while you practice the falloff back dive until you are absolutely confident.

Reverse dives

takeoff (above)
You can use a one- or two-foot takeoff although the two-foot version is preferable.
1 Kick away from the board with one foot. As you move away, throw your arms over your head.
2 Leave the board with both feet. Lift your hips high and bring your arms into the cross position. Drop your shoulders and arch your body.

reverse dive straight
(left)
This is a back dive with a forward takeoff. Drive off from the board, arms raised. Lift your chest. Keep your head up so that your legs and thighs follow in an upward movement. Widen your hands out into the cross position. At the crest, drop your head back. Drop toward the water and enter vertically.

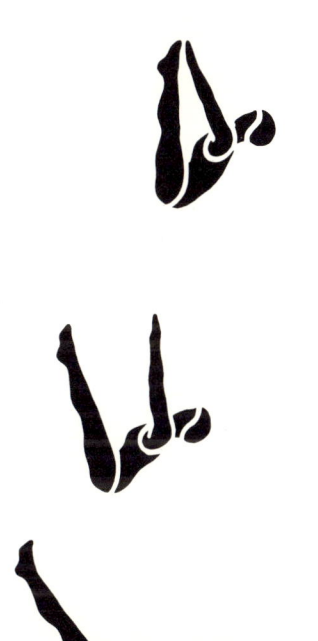

reverse dive, pike (above)
Drive off from the board. As you rise, bend at the hips and pike. Reach back with your arms and stretch for the water.

Inward dives

This inward dive takes off from the same position as a straight back dive. But in the air the actions are the same as a forward pike. Basically you are performing the dive inward, toward the board. In fact because you are diving so close to the board you must take care that you jump up and well away from the board to avoid injury.

practice
Practice the two dives below until you are confident of clearing the board.
1 Start this standing back jump from one corner of the board for safety. Jump up and diagonally away from the board. Then try from the center of the board.

2 Practice this inward pike, again starting from a corner. Flex your ankles and knees and jump off the board upward and diagonally. Bend to form a pike. Try again, from the center of the board.

inward dive, piked (right)
Drive up and out from the board. Keep your head up. Bend at the hips and pike. Your hips should be higher than your shoulders. Touch your toes with your fingertips. Bring your legs up. Stretch your arms through the cross position and over your head. Enter the water vertically, keeping toes pointed.

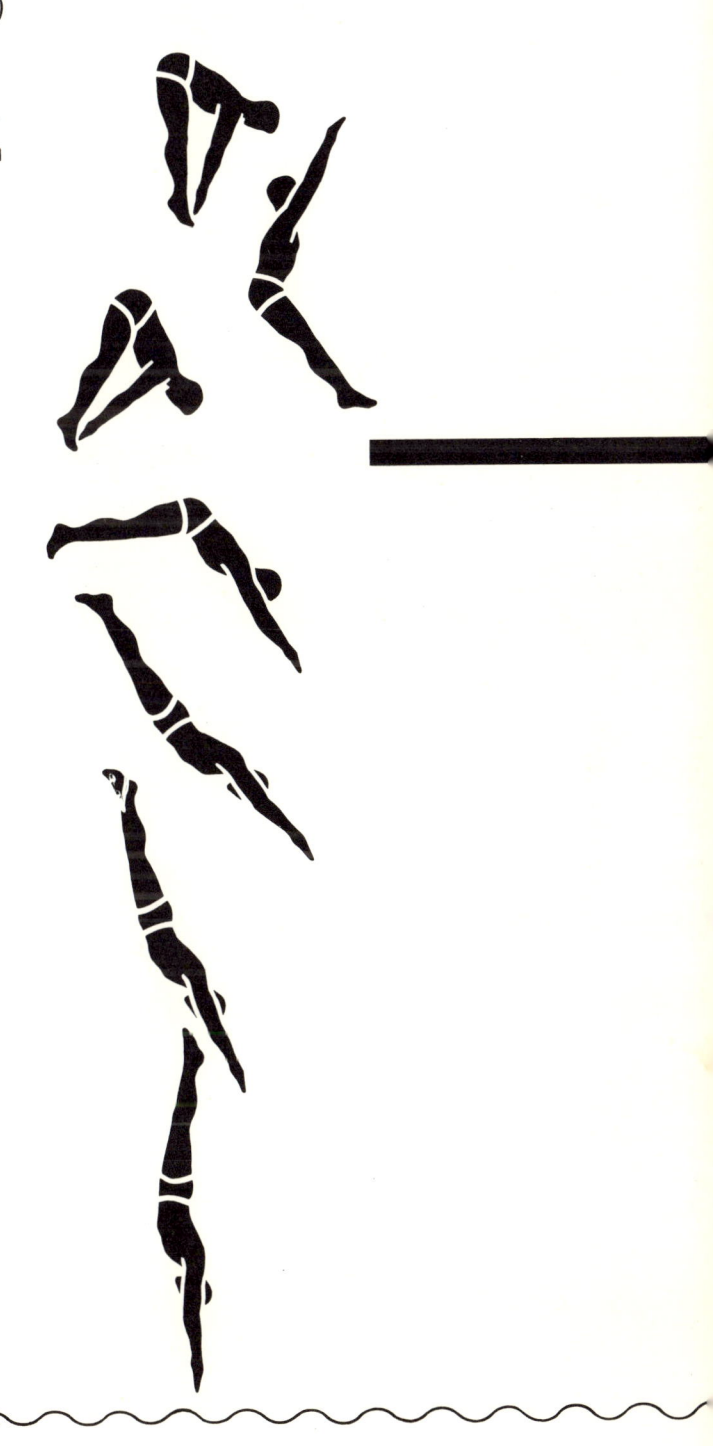

Twist dives

forward dive, half twist
This is a beautiful but difficult dive. It needs very good balance. Leave the board in a vertical position. Spread your arms horizontally into the cross or swan position. Point your arms at the water and rotate your body to the right. Turn until your back is to the water. Stretch your arms ahead to enter the water.

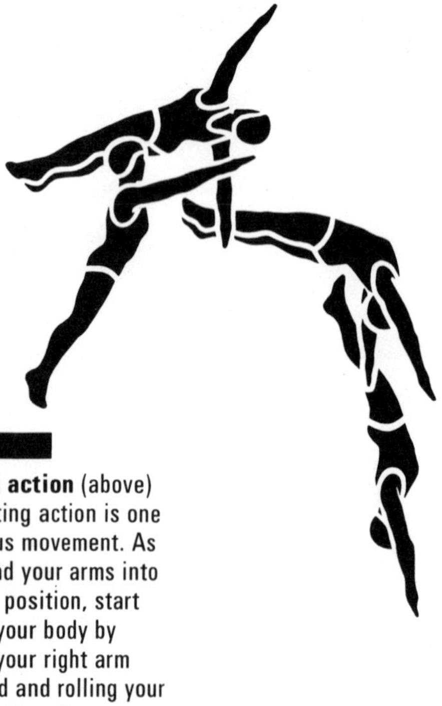

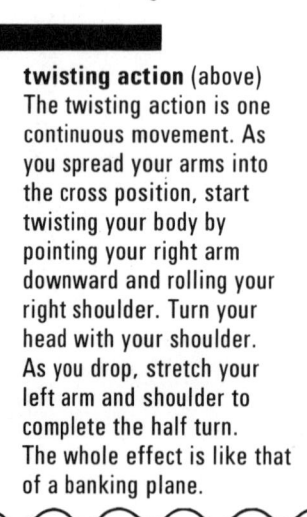

twisting action (above)
The twisting action is one continuous movement. As you spread your arms into the cross position, start twisting your body by pointing your right arm downward and rolling your right shoulder. Turn your head with your shoulder. As you drop, stretch your left arm and shoulder to complete the half turn. The whole effect is like that of a banking plane.

reverse dive, half twist (right)
Leave the board in the same way as for the forward twist. Move into the cross position but reverse the twist so that you enter the water facing away from the board, unlike a normal reverse dive.

practice (above)
This simple exercise will help you to practice the twist. Stand on the board, facing the water. Jump into the air. Keeping your elbows bent and arms against your chest, twist to the right. Keep your toes pointed and let your head follow the twist. Enter the water feet first.
You must wear a swimming cap when learning the twist dives.

Pike and tuck dives

pike drill
This exercise will help you both to learn the mechanics of the pike and to develop strong stomach muscles. Jump off the board, arms up. Keep your head up and toes pointed. Using your stomach muscles, bring your legs up horizontally. Bend at the hips and touch your toes. Straighten your legs and enter the water, arms at your sides, toes pointed.

forward pike (jackknife)
To perform this well you need a smooth approach, good body control, and strong stomach muscles. Leave the board vertically, arms raised. Near the top of the dive, drive your hips up behind you and bring your legs slightly forward. Touch your toes. Keep your head up and back flat. Bring your legs into line with your back. Bring your arms forward for entry.

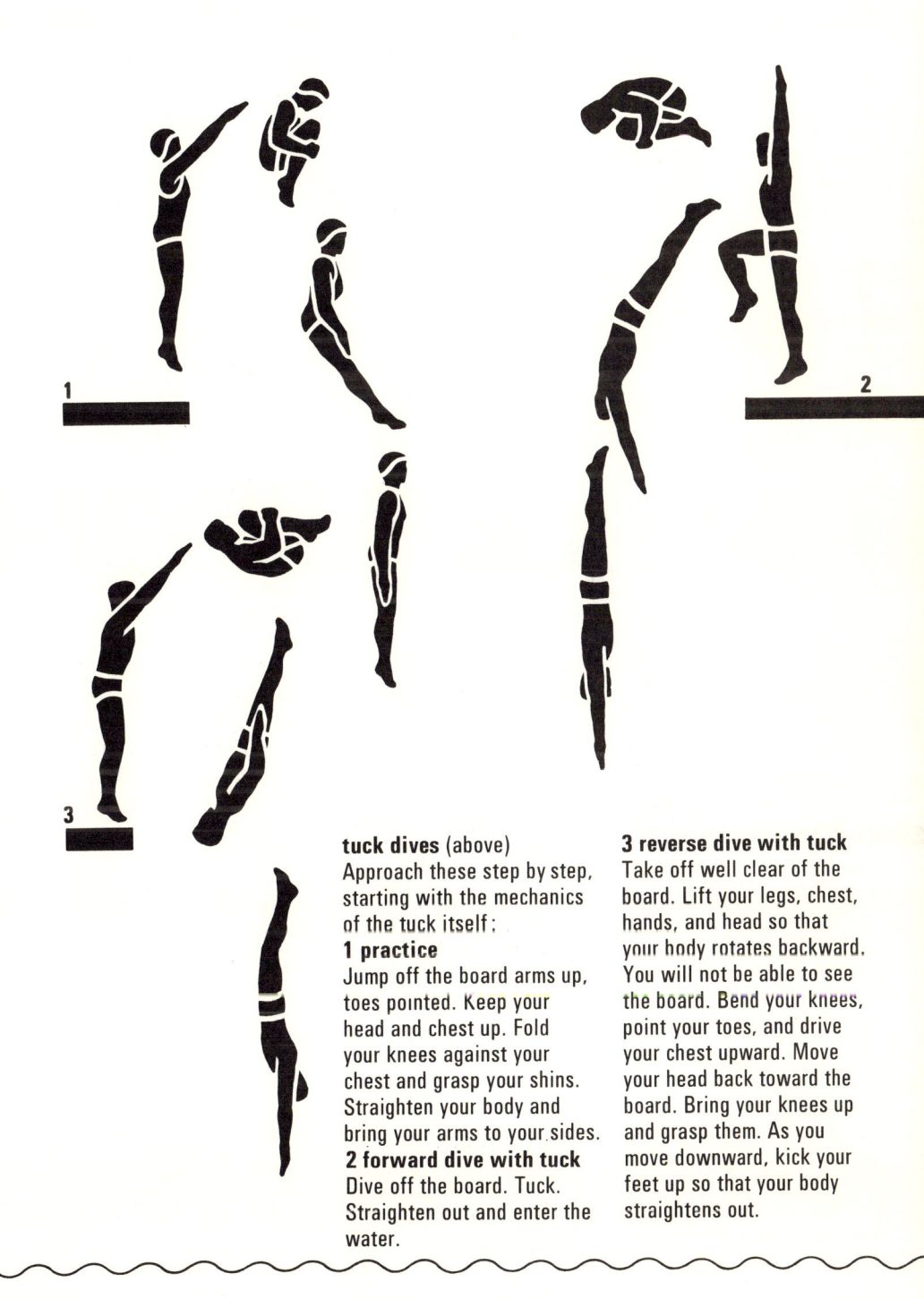

tuck dives (above)
Approach these step by step, starting with the mechanics of the tuck itself:
1 practice
Jump off the board arms up, toes pointed. Keep your head and chest up. Fold your knees against your chest and grasp your shins. Straighten your body and bring your arms to your sides.
2 forward dive with tuck
Dive off the board. Tuck. Straighten out and enter the water.

3 reverse dive with tuck
Take off well clear of the board. Lift your legs, chest, hands, and head so that your body rotates backward. You will not be able to see the board. Bend your knees, point your toes, and drive your chest upward. Move your head back toward the board. Bring your knees up and grasp them. As you move downward, kick your feet up so that your body straightens out.

Somersault dives

Once you have perfected the basic dives, you can begin to experiment with some of the beautiful but more advanced dives on this page. The basic requirements still hold good: you need balance, body control, and a fine sense of timing. And you need confidence. Before attempting to do a somersault in the air, practice with a coach, somersaulting into the water from the side of the pool. Once you have mastered the wheel-like spinning action that makes a good somersault, then you can move onto the board.

forward 1½ somersault, tuck

The main points to watch for in a front somersault tuck are the positions of the head, shoulders, and feet. Basically your tuck position needs to be much tighter than normal. Keep your knees slightly apart and bring your head and shoulders down toward your knees rather than holding your knees up to your chest. In effect a forward tucked somersault is a tight, rotating movement in which the head and shoulders take the lead. Your toes should be pointed in the direction in which you are spinning and you should get the feel that you are chasing your toes.

reverse somersault, straight
Lift your legs and thighs and drive your chest, hands, and head up into the high point of the dive. Let your head and arms take you through the spinning motion.

inward 1½ somersault, pike
For this dive wait until you are sufficiently clear of the board before moving into your somersault. Concentrate on pushing your hips well over your head to get a good spinning motion.

Competition diving

Like swimming, diving goes back far in history and it is impossible to say when man first began entering water headfirst. Competitive diving first began at the end of the 19th century but conditions were crude and positively dangerous by today's standards. Divers were expected to plunge into murky depths from a narrow plank perched on often rickety staging. Today diving boards are subject to strict regulations and a minimum depth of water is required to surround the board and diving area.

Competition diving was first recognized at the 1904 Olympic Games when it was won by the United States. In 1912 there were three diving events for men, and women made their first Olympic diving appearance. Today competitive diving is separated into men's and women's springboard and highboard events. Competition diving has become not only a highly skilled sport but also a stunning display of aerial acrobatics.

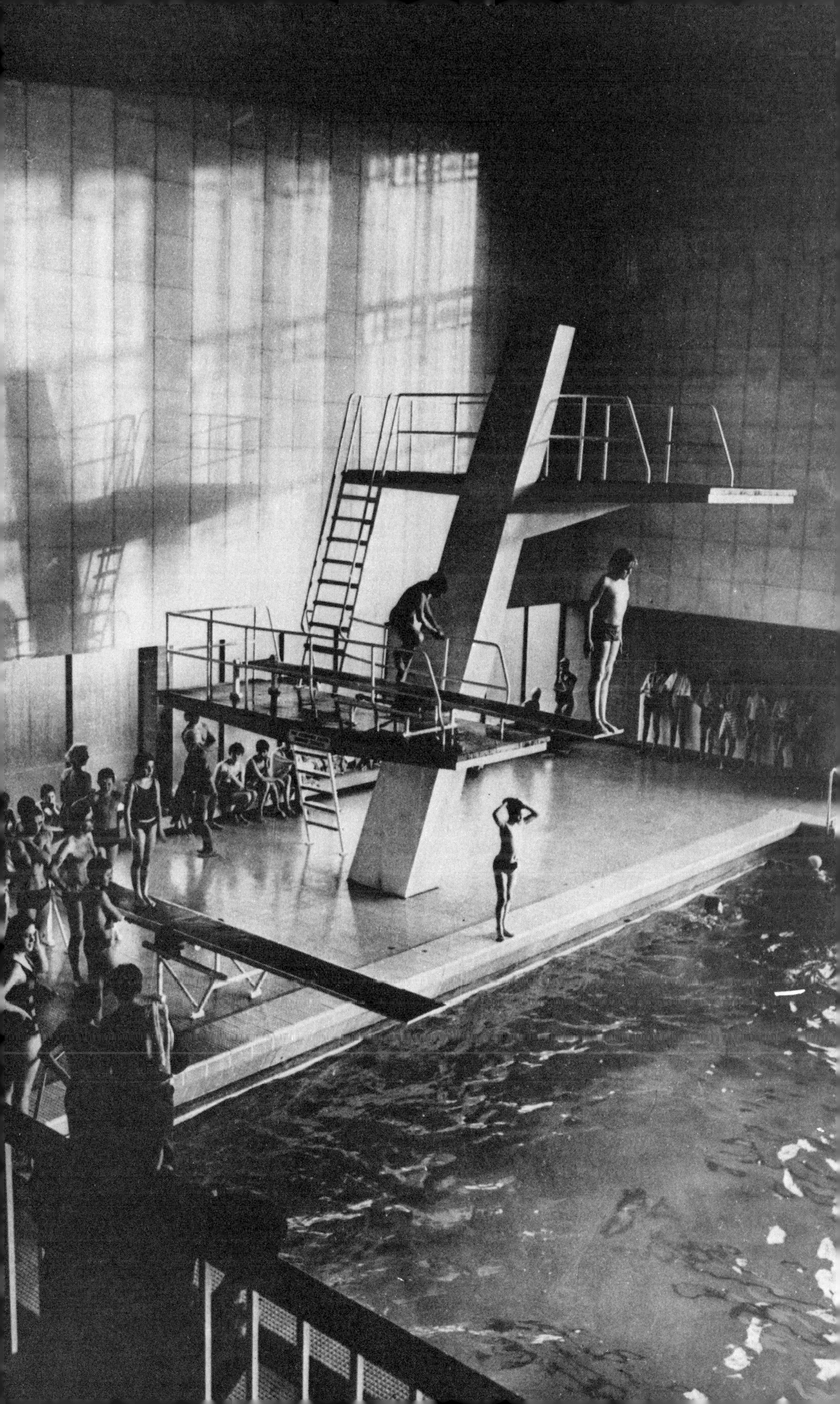

Rules

Competitive diving is separated into men's and women's springboard and highboard events. Competitors perform a set number of compulsory and voluntary dives, each of which is marked. A competition is won by the competitor with most marks.

officials
Competitions are judged by a panel consisting of a referee and diving judges. The referee controls the competition and supervises the judges.
The judges (usually five or seven in major international competitions) are positioned separately on both sides of the diving board or, if that is not possible, together on one side of the board. After each dive, each judge gives his mark when the referee signals.
Marks are recorded by two secretaries, who also record the minutes of the competition.

Springboards
Springboards are 1m (3ft 3in) or 3m (9ft 9in) high, with a fulcrum that may be adjusted by the competitors.

diving apparatus
Highboard diving platforms and springboards are provided at the heights shown.
Platforms must be rigid and covered with a resilient surface of approved nonslip material. Springboards must be made of an aluminum extrusion.
Mechanical agitation of the water's surface aids divers. Illumination must not cause glare.

1 platform
a height	b length	c width	d to pool edge
10m	6m	2m	1.50m
33ft	19ft 6ins	6ft 6ins	4ft 11ins

2 platform
e height	f length	g width	h to pool edge
7.50m	6m	1.50m	1.50m
24ft 5ins	19ft 6ins	4ft 11ins	4ft 11ins

3 platform
i height	j length	k width	l to pool edge
5m	6m	1.50m	1.25m
16ft 3ins	19ft 6ins	4ft 11ins	4ft 1in

4 platform
m height	n length	o width	p to pool edge
3m	5m	0.80m	1.25m
9ft 9ins	16ft 3ins	2ft 8ins	4ft 1in

5 springboard
q height	r length	s width	t to pool edge
1m	5m	0.50m	1.50m
3ft 3ins	16ft 3ins	1ft 8ins	4ft 11ins

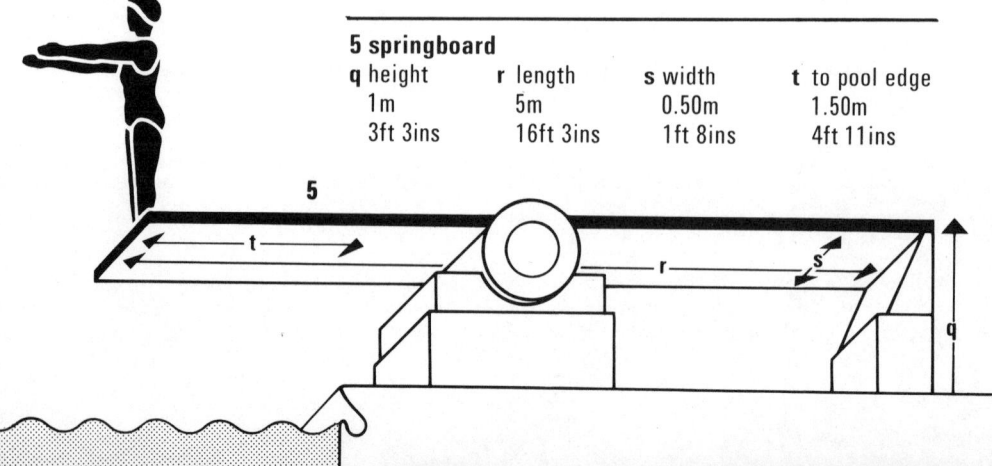

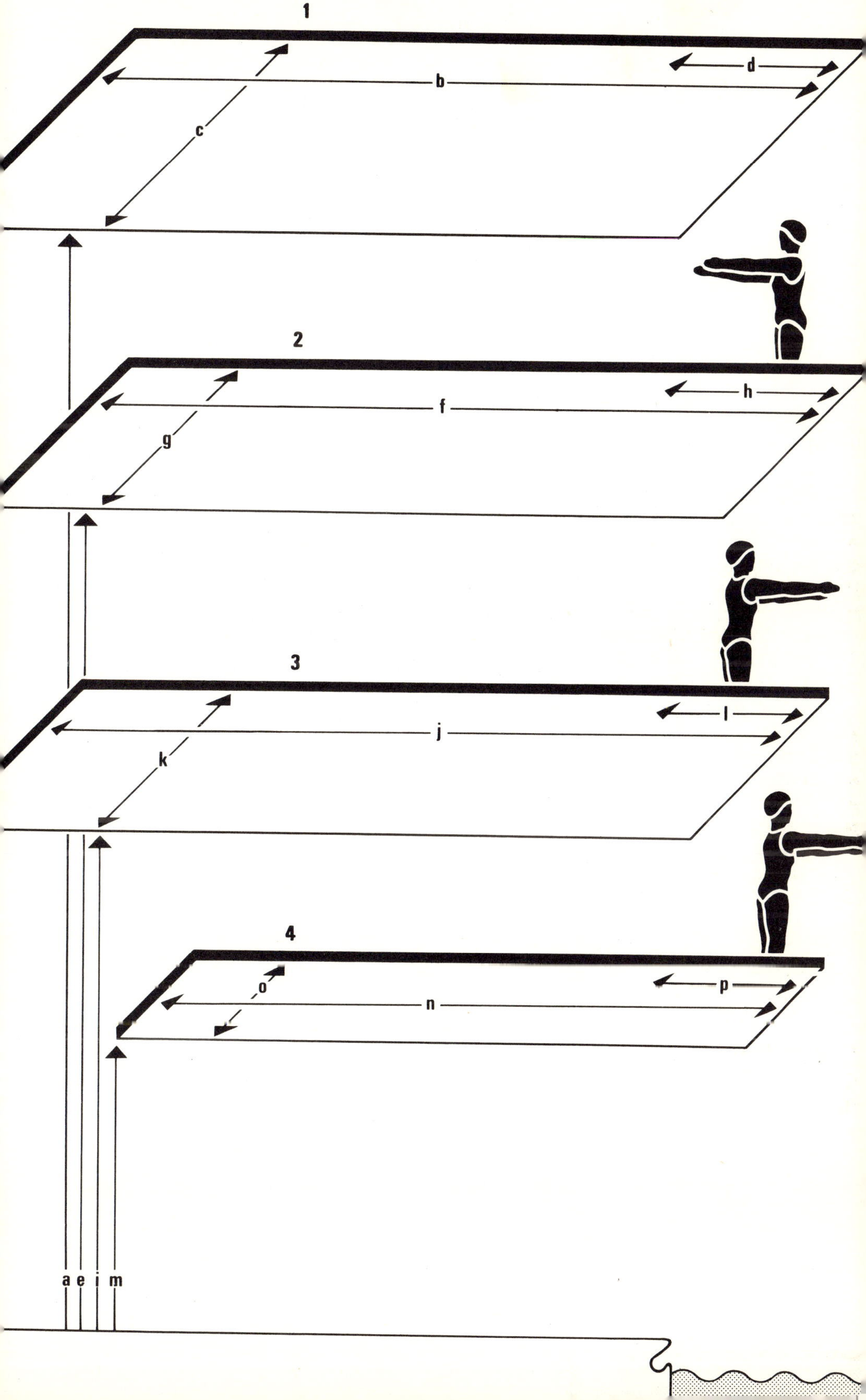

1
b
c
d
2
f
g
h
3
j
k
l
4
n
o
p
a
e
i
m

twist dives

reverse dives

inward dives

groups of dives
There are six official groups of dives:
Forward dives (body facing the water)
Backward dives (body facing the platform)
Reverse dives (body facing the water)
Inward dives (body facing the platform)
Twist dives
Armstand dives

preliminary contests
Preliminary contests in the Olympic Games and World Championships are held when there are more than 16 competitors.
In springboard events a preliminary contest consists of 11 dives for men and 10 for women.
In highboard events 10 dives are required for men and eight for women.
In both competitions the same dives must be performed in the final as in the preliminary contest. The eight divers with the most points in the preliminary contest qualify for the final.

events
men's springboard
Men's springboard events consist of five required dives, and six voluntary dives selected from five groups.
The required dives are: a forward dive, a backward dive, a reverse dive, an inward dive, and a forward dive with a half twist. They may be performed straight, piked, or with tuck.

women's springboard
Women's springboard events consist of five required dives, and five voluntary dives selected from five groups. The required dives are the same as for the men's springboard events.
men's highboard
Men's highboard events consist of four voluntary dives with a maximum total degree of difficulty of 7.5, and six voluntary dives without limit.
In each section, each dive must be selected from a different group.
The dives may be performed from either the intermediate or the 10m (33ft) platform.
women's highboard
Women's highboard events consist of four voluntary dives with a maximum total degree of difficulty of 7.5, and four voluntary dives without limit.
In each section, each dive must be selected from a different group.
Dives may be performed from either the intermediate or the 10m (33ft) platform.
notification of dives
Before the competition each competitor must give the diving secretaries full information about each of his dives, including a written description.
A dive can be performed in three positions: straight, piked, and tucked. Difficult twist dives may be performed in any position.

armstand dives

backward dives

forward dives

Rules

1

judging dives
The judges consider the run, takeoff, flight, and entry, but not the approach to the starting position.

2

starting positions
Divers may take off from a backward (**1**), forward (**2**), or armstand (**3**) position. Forward takeoff dives may be performed either standing or running.

3

standing dives
The starting position for a standing dive is assumed when the diver stands on the front end of the board or platform.
The body must be straight, head erect, arms straight and to the sides or above the head. The arm swing commences when the arms leave the starting position.

4

5

6

the execution
During the flight (passage through the air) the body may be straight, with pike, or with tuck. The position of the arms is the choice of the diver.
straight (4)
The body must not be bent at the knees or hips; the feet must be together and the toes pointed.

with pike (5)
The body must be bent at the hips, the legs straight at the knees and the toes pointed.
with tuck (6)
The whole body must be bunched, with the knees together, the hands on the lower legs, and the toes pointed.

straight dives with twist
The twist must not be manifestly made from the board. In pike dives with twist, the twist must follow the pike. In somersault dives with twist, the twist may be performed at any time. The twist must be within 90° of that announced or the dive will be declared a failure.

running dives
The starting position for a running dive is assumed when the diver is ready to take the first step of his run.

The run must be smooth, straight, and without hesitation, and must consist of at least four steps, including the takeoff from one or both feet.
The takeoff must be bold, reasonably high, and confident.
In a standing dive the diver must not bounce on the board.
In an armstand dive there must be a steady balance in the straight position.
In a running dive from the springboard the takeoff must be from both feet simultaneously; from fixed boards it may be from one foot.

the entry
The body must always be vertical or near vertical on entering the water. The body must be straight and the toes pointed.
headfirst entries (7)
The arms must be stretched above the head and in line with the body; the hands must be close together.

feetfirst entries (8)
The arms must be close to the body; there must be no bending at the elbows.
finish
The dive is considered finished when the whole body is completely under the surface of the water.

scoring
Each judge awards a mark in points and half points from 0–10 for each dive. The secretaries cancel the judges' highest and lowest marks, total the remainder, and multiply by the degree of difficulty to give the score for the dive.
A dive other than that announced is a failed dive and scores no points.
A dive performed in a position other than that announced is deemed unsatisfactory and scores a maximum of two points.
A dive spoiled by exceptional circumstances may, with the referee's permission, be repeated.
result
An event is won by the competitor scoring the most points. A tie is declared if two divers have equal points.
Points may be deducted for loss of balance, restarting, touching the end of the board, diving to the side of the direct line of flight, or lifting both feet from the board when preparing for a backward takeoff

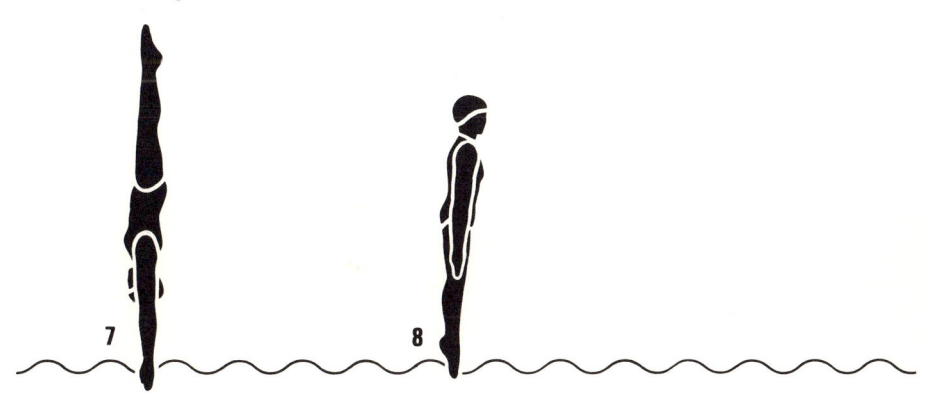

Underwater swimming

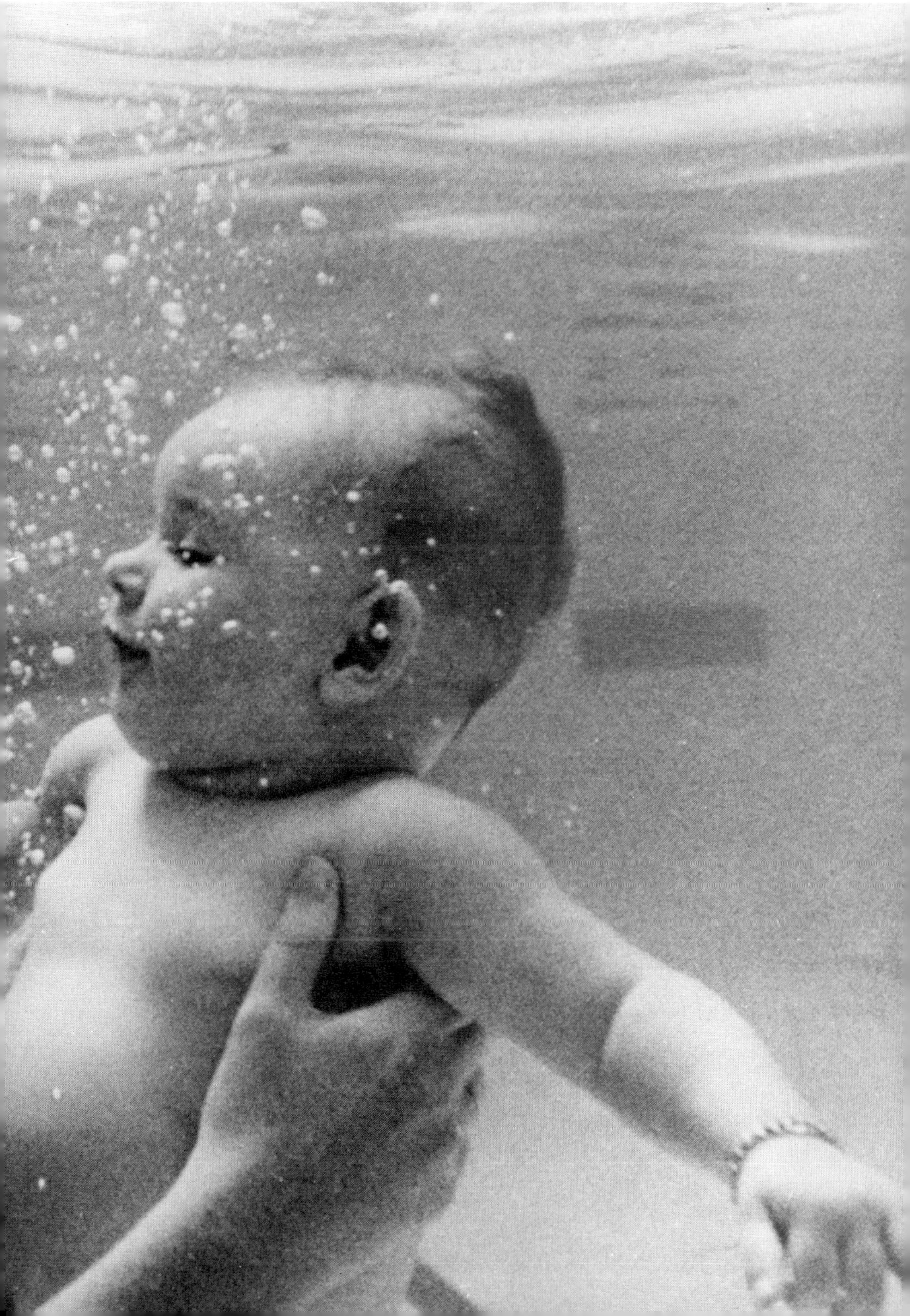

Underwater swimming

The underwater world is both fantastic and indescribably beautiful. It is a changing, moving world of great and varying depths ranging from the shallow shore waters to the silent ocean depths and is inhabited by innumerable plants and animals quite unlike those on land. Although water covers two thirds of the world's surface, this mysterious world is still relatively unexplored. Men have been attracted to the depths for many centuries, but only in the last 30 years has it become safe for the ordinary person to venture under the surface.

In 1943 the Frenchmen Jacques Yves Cousteau and Emil Gagnan developed a valve for releasing compressed air. This opened the gates to underwater exploration and since then, inspired by fascinating films on television and in the cinema, many thousands of people have been able to take part in the new and exciting pastime of underwater swimming.

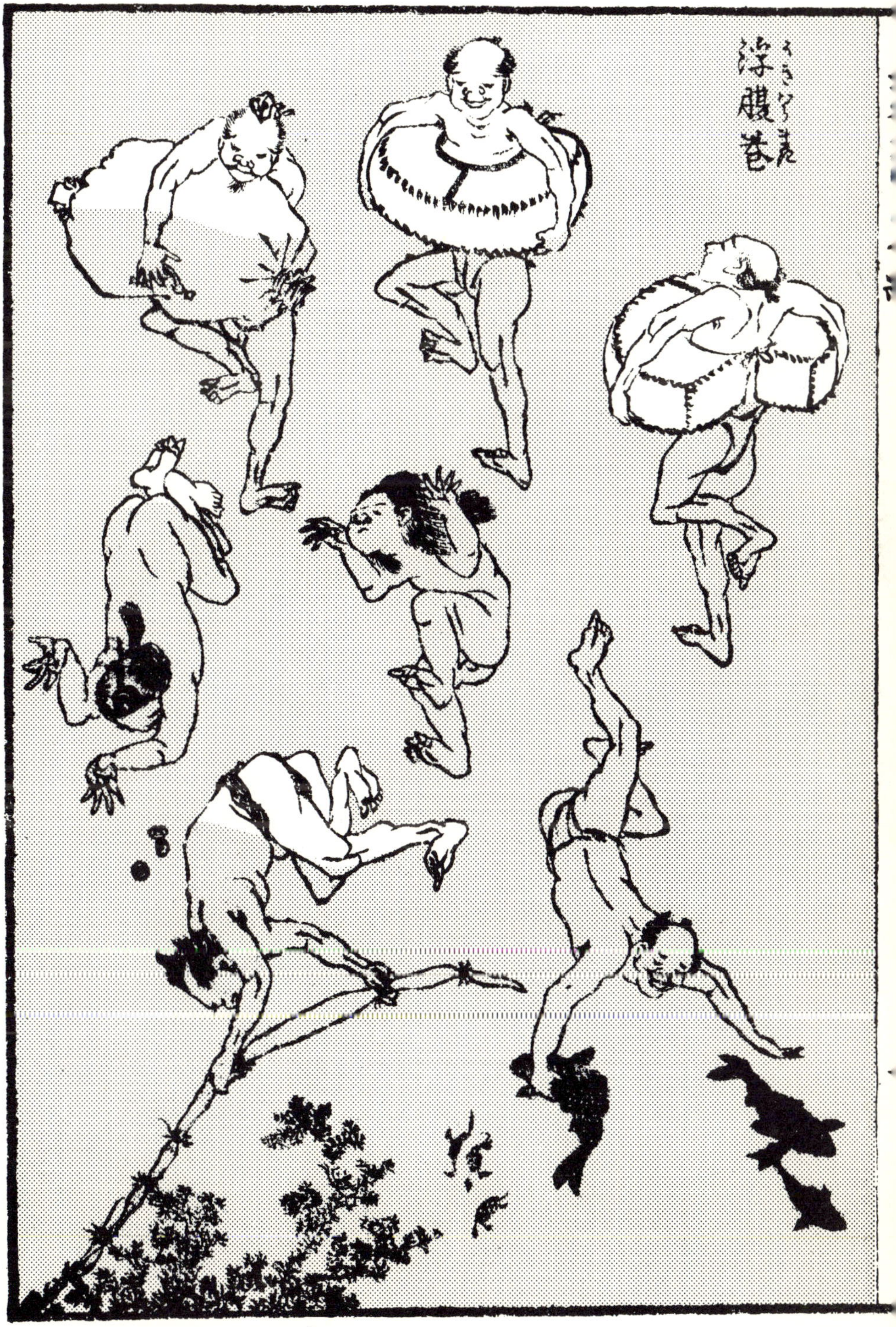
浮腹巻

Equipment

Choose your equipment carefully. To start with, all you really need is a mask, fins, and a snorkel. Never use ear plugs or nose clips; they are unnecessary and also dangerous. And remember one cardinal rule—never dive alone, always dive with a partner.

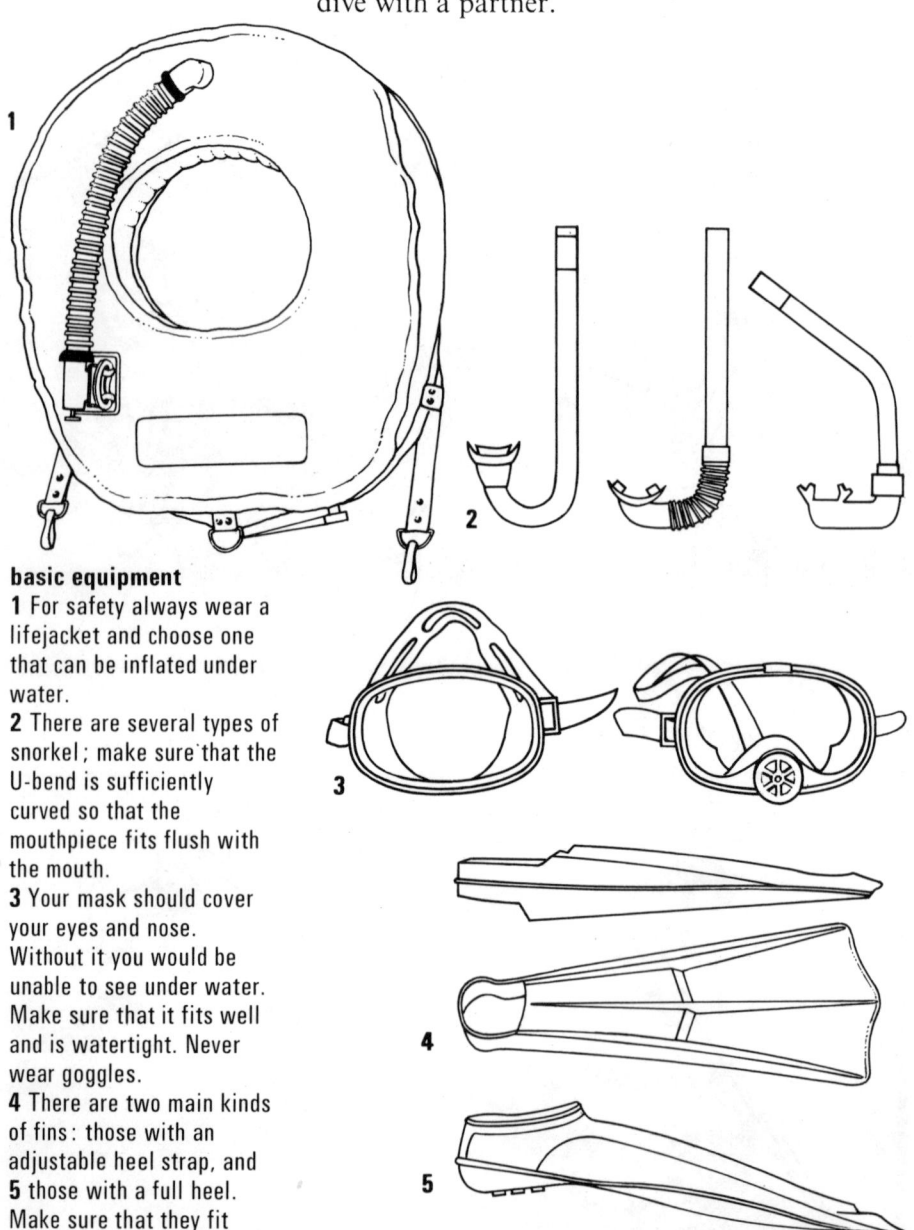

basic equipment
1 For safety always wear a lifejacket and choose one that can be inflated under water.
2 There are several types of snorkel; make sure that the U-bend is sufficiently curved so that the mouthpiece fits flush with the mouth.
3 Your mask should cover your eyes and nose. Without it you would be unable to see under water. Make sure that it fits well and is watertight. Never wear goggles.
4 There are two main kinds of fins: those with an adjustable heel strap, and
5 those with a full heel. Make sure that they fit comfortably and do not rub.

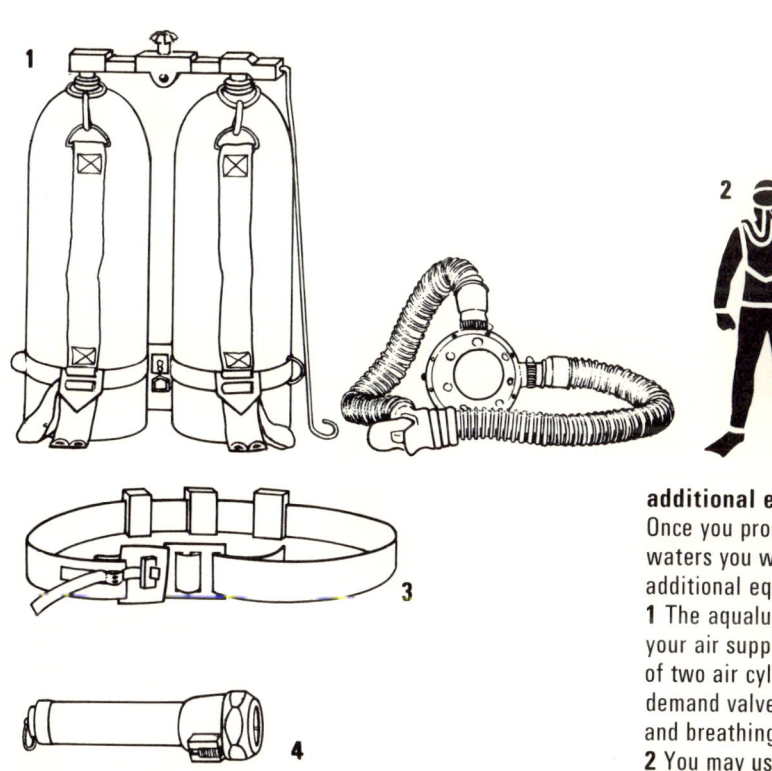

additional equipment
Once you progress to deeper waters you will need additional equipment.
1 The aqualung provides your air supply. It consists of two air cylinders, a demand valve or regulator, and breathing tubes.
2 You may use a diving suit. There are two kinds—the traditional watertight rubber suit or the neoprene wet suit. This is worn next to the skin but allows a layer of water to enter that insulates you against cold.
3 Use a weight belt to counter the buoyancy of the wet suit and air cylinders.
4 An underwater torch is useful, and
5 a knife can prove invaluable.

Necessary skills

To skindive with safety and confidence you do need a certain amount of competence in water. On this page we show a few of the skills that you will need and we also suggest various tests that you can use to measure your ability. Remember, however, that you must always pay attention to safety. Although you can teach yourself to snorkel dive, it is better and safer to join a club and learn with the experts. Try all the suggestions on this page without using equipment.

skills
1 Practice the crawl or flutter kick, which is the basis of swimming with fins; aim for a slow kick from the hips. Keep your feet below the surface to avoid splashing.
2 Make sure that you can do the breaststroke kick, used for underwater swimming without fins.
3 Swim for 180m (585ft) without stopping; you should swim slowly but continuously.
4 Tread water for three minutes with your hands below water, and
5 for one minute with your hands above water.
6 Swim under water for at least 10m (33ft).

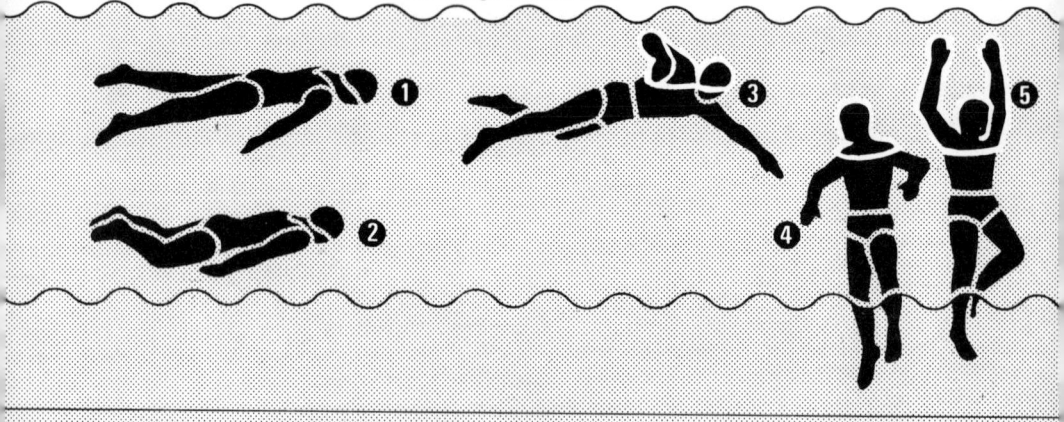

7 Float on your back for at least one minute, and on your front, face down; take a deep breath before starting and float for as long as you can hold your breath.
8 Jump into 2.5m (8ft) of water, feet first; hold your nose as you descend, blowing air out gently through your nostrils against your fingers; this exercise, known as equalizing, balances the air pressure in your ears and nose against that of the water.
9 Dive headfirst into deep water;
10 breathe out through partly closed nostrils, and
11 pick up a 2kg (5lb) weight from the bottom.

Basics

11m

22m

pressure
At sea level, air pressure is 14.7lb per square inch, or one atmosphere. Water is roughly 800 times heavier than air and only 11m (33ft) down it also exerts a pressure of 14.7lb psi. Therefore when a swimmer is 11m (33ft) down he is subject to two atmospheres or 29.5lb psi. One more atmosphere is added every additional 11m (33ft). Although serious disorders such as the bends or nitrogen narcosis are suffered only by deep-sea divers, pressure can also affect skindivers. Ear ache

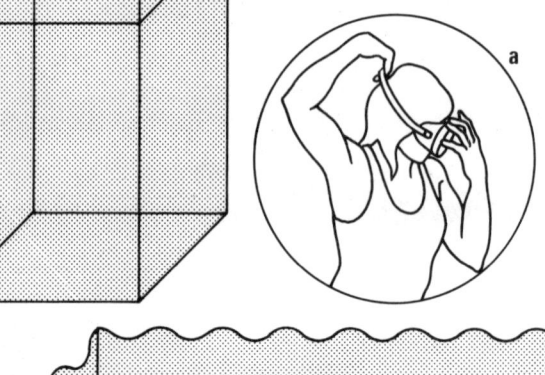

putting the mask on
Place your mask in position on your face and breathe in. If it is air tight it will stay in place. Then pull the strap down over the back of your head (**a**). Never put the strap on first and pull the mask into place.
You should practice putting your diving equipment on under water. When you put your mask on under water it will naturally be full of water. To clear it, hold it against your face and exhale hard through your nose.

is a common problem. As you descend, water pressure pushes onto the ear drum. You must equalize this pressure to prevent a burst ear drum. The best way is to yawn, swallow or blow gently through closed nostrils. Never dive with a cold or wearing ear plugs. Pressure can also cause mask squeeze, which leads to bruising. To avoid this, blow into the mask as you descend. The demand valve will automatically adjust the internal pressure to that outside but do not descend or surface too quickly.

clearing mask and snorkel
If your mask fills with water near the surface, raise your head above water, pull the bottom of the mask away from your face, and let the water drain out. But if it happens in deeper water, you should tilt your head back and exhale hard through your nose (**b**). The air will go to the top of the mask and the water will be forced out through the bottom. If you are swimming horizontally when your mask floods, roll to one side until you are virtually on your back, press the upper part of your mask, and again exhale through your nose (**c**). When you use a snorkel under the surface, the tube fills with water. But this will not enter your mouth unless you inhale. To clear your snorkel, rise to the surface and blow sharply through the mouthpiece (**d**).

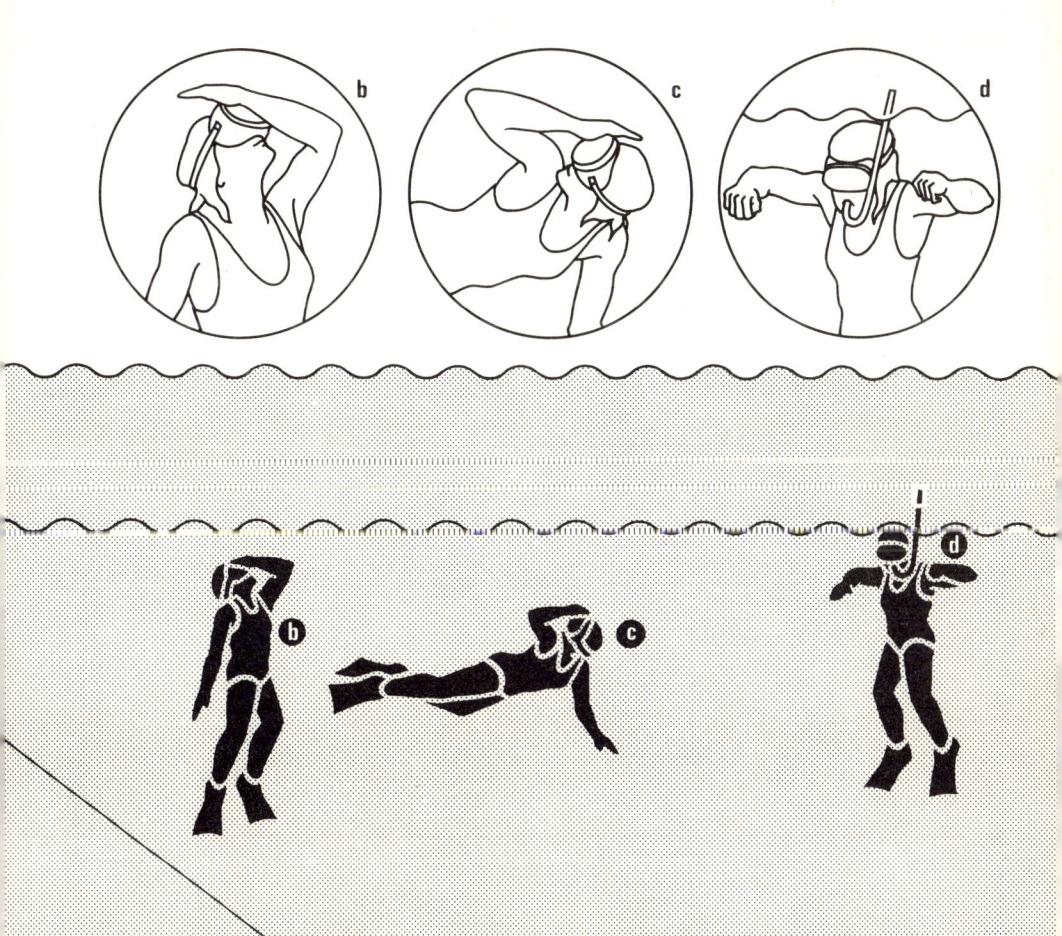

Maneuvers

depth of dive
When you are snorkel diving the depth of your dive depends partly on how long you can hold your breath, and partly on the effects of pressure. Below 6m (20ft), because of the reduced volume of your lungs, the body loses its natural buoyancy and you will tend to sink. You must take this into account when making dives of more than 6m (20ft), as you will need extra effort to fin up to a point where your body regains its buoyancy. Before making a dive you should take two or three deep breaths. Never hyperventilate, or take too many rapid breaths. To do so can lead to anoxia, or lack of oxygen, which can be fatal. Learn to relax under water, moving as effortlessly as possible. You will conserve oxygen and gradually lengthen your time under water.

entry

To get into the water when you are wearing diving equipment, hold your mask in place and either
1 fall in backward, shoulders first, or
2 jump in legs astride. Kick your legs together as you enter.
Once in the water use a surface dive to submerge.

You can do this
3 headfirst by jackknifing at the hips. Keep your **arms by your sides and** straighten your legs, and their weight will drive you down.
4 Alternatively you can make a feetfirst surface dive, which is probably easier if you are wearing fins. Start by treading water. Bring your arms to your sides and kick your legs together. This will bring your head and shoulders out of the water. As you begin to sink, bring your arms up to help you descend. Pull your knees to your chest and lower your head so that your body rotates. Straighten out and swim.

Underwater signals

Sight and sound are affected dramatically by water. Objects appear to be nearer and larger than they actually are and sound travels much faster than on land. Noise can be heard from quite far away but it is hard to tell from which direction it is coming. As a result it is difficult for divers to communicate with each other under water and international hand signals have been developed for essential information.

communication
Some of the most important hand signals are:
1 I am out of breath. The diver moves his hands from side to side at chest level.
2 I have no air. The diver touches his mouthpiece repeatedly with cupped fingers.
3 Go up, or I am going up. This is either an order given, or a statement made, at the end of a dive. The fingers are clenched and thumb pointed upward.
4 Go down or I am going down. Again this is either an order or a statement but it is made at the beginning of a dive. The fingers are clenched and the thumb pointed downward.
5 Something is wrong. This does not necessarily mean an emergency but merely indicates that things are not right. The hand is held outward, palm down, and is moved gently up and down.
6 Stop, stay where you are. For this command the hand is held up, palm outward.

7 I am on reserve/I have 30 ats left in my cylinder. The fist is clenched, thumb over the fingers, and held at eye level.

8 I cannot pull my reserve. This indicates that the diver needs help to pull his reserve lever. The fist is again clenched and rotated from side to side.

9 Danger. The diver draws his finger across his throat and points to the source of the danger.

10 I am OK. The diver holds his hand up, thumb and index finger touching.

11 I need assistance. This signal is given on the surface. The diver holds his arm up, fist clenched, and waves it slowly from side to side indicating that he wants to be picked up.

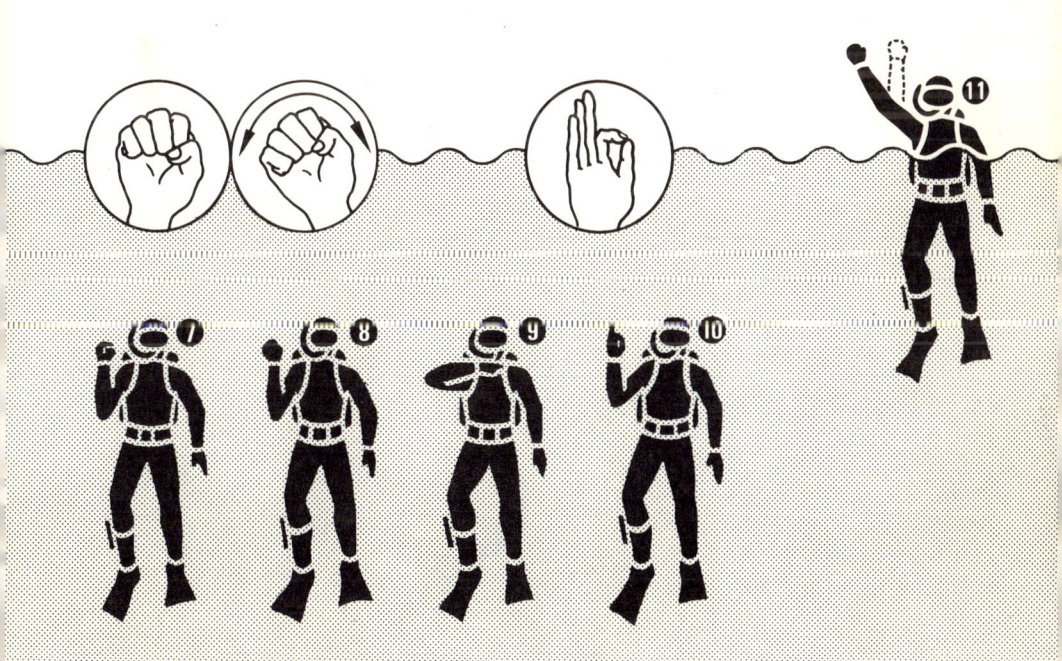

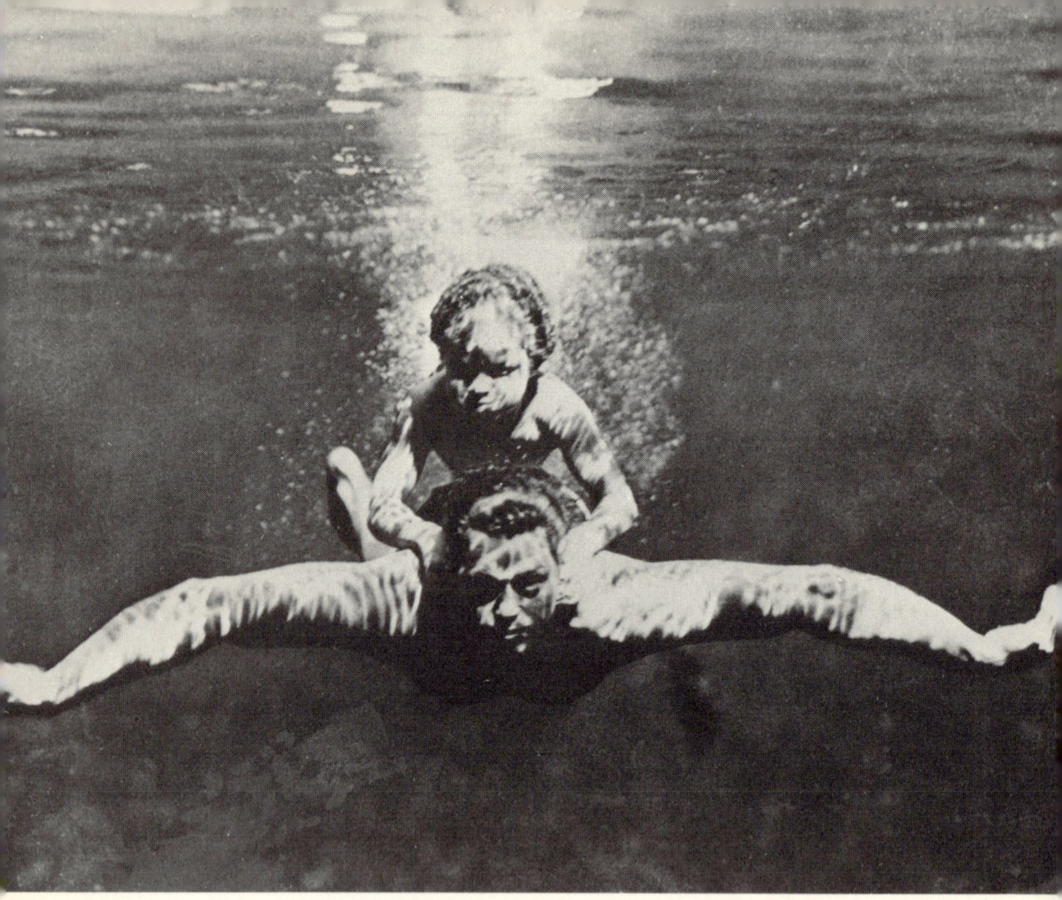

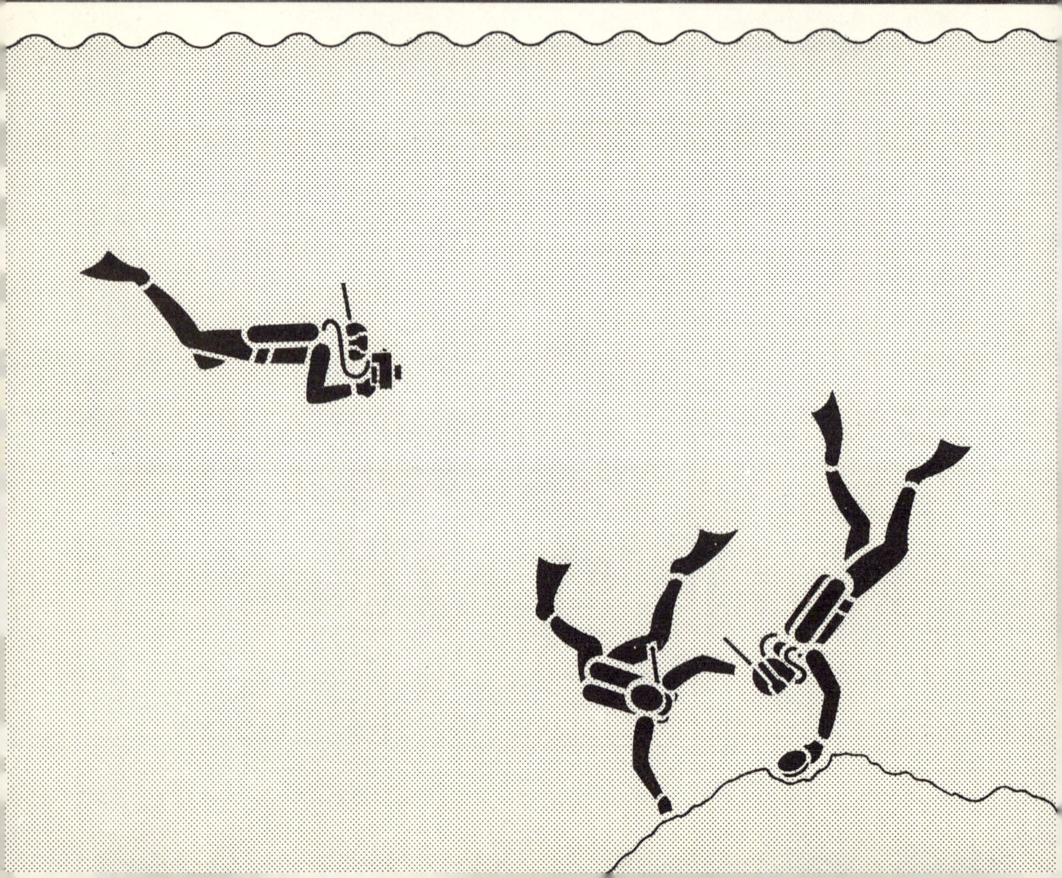

Underwater activities

Once you feel at home under the water there are any number of fascinating activities to choose from. Underwater photography or marine biology are just two examples. Archeology is another, as the seas and rivers hold many rewarding finds from old wrecks and buried towns and villages. And spearfishing can provide an exciting challenge for the sportsman, but make sure that your motive is sport and not just killing for killing's sake.

equipment
For underwater photography you will need a special camera and you should use a wide-angled lens. The best photographs are those taken near the surface in strong sunlight. Very little equipment is needed for underwater archeology or marine biology. Your findings are all around you. But you may find a camera useful for keeping records or even just a slate and pencil. There is a wide variety of equipment available for the spearfisher—knives, spears, and even powerful guns, although these last are illegal in many waters. For this activity you should pay particular attention to safety.

Water safety

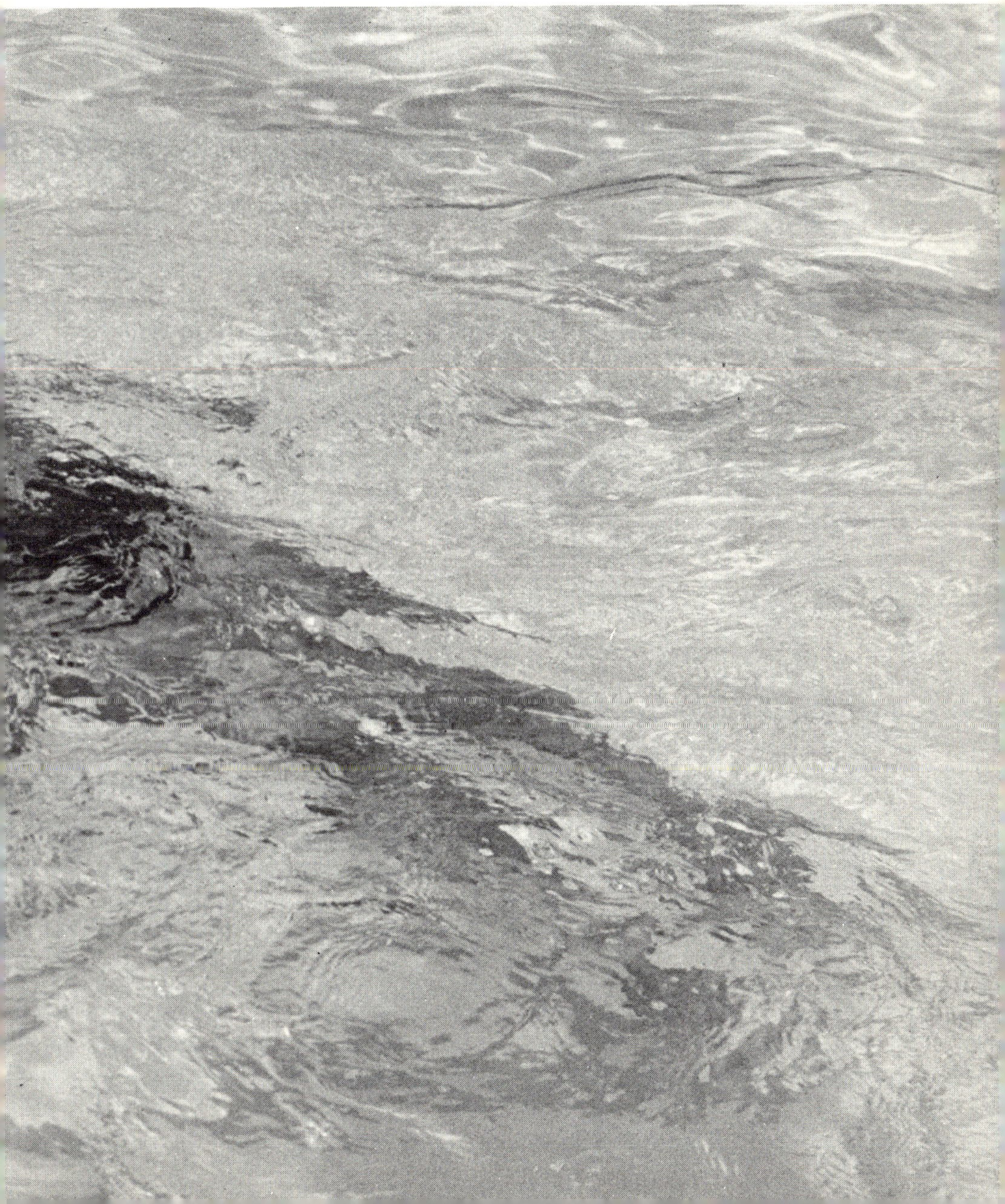

Water safety

Hundreds of people drown each year—in swimming pools, in rivers, or in the sea. But most tragic of all is that in the majority of cases these accidents should never have happened. By following various safety precautions drowning accidents can be avoided.

The most sensible precaution of all is to learn to swim properly and to avoid taking unnecessary risks. But for swimmers and nonswimmers alike fooling around in water is stupid and could cost someone else his life. In general it is best to swim with friends or to bathe in a crowd. If an accident happens there is then always someone around to help.

Respect the water and avoid swimming where there is a deeply shelving beach, fast-running currents, or weed-infested waters. If you do get entangled in weeds, move gently in the direction of the weeds so that you drift out of them. Pay attention to the tides, for it is only too easy to be cut off from land. If you are, then swim horizontally to the tide, not against it. In rivers it is safest to stay waist deep, and in the sea to swim parallel to the shore. Always obey warning signals such as red flags—there is good reason for them to be there.

Physical fitness is important—illness and cramp are common causes of accidents. No one should swim with a cold, a skin infection, or ear trouble. Nor should anyone swim after a meal. Another danger is overconfidence. No swimmer should overestimate his ability—too many swimmers have died from exhaustion.

In any emergency, panic is probably the most dangerous factor of all. Ideally anyone who swims should learn some of the special skills needed in an emergency—how to get into water in a hurry, how to float and swim under water, and how to get out of water. In addition lifesaving skills such as artificial respiration can be invaluable. Armed with sense and training anyone can avoid swimming tragedies.

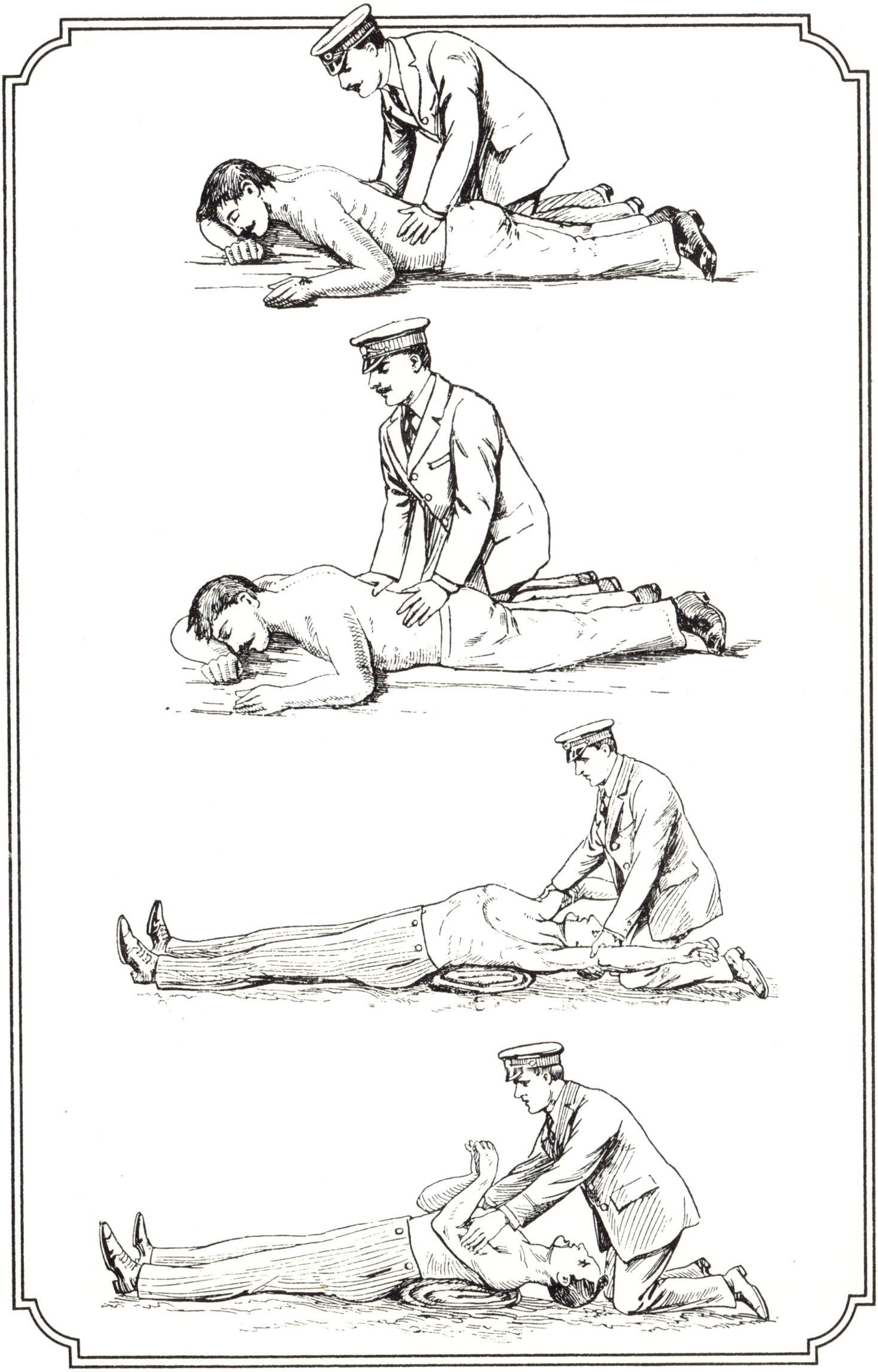

Forced entry

feetfirst entry
If you are forced to enter water from a height, always go in feetfirst, particularly if you are an inexperienced swimmer or entering shallow or unknown water. This is a much safer way of entering water than a headfirst dive. The simplest method (**a**) is to step from the height rather than jump. Looking straight ahead, step forward sharply with one foot and quickly move the other to join it. Keep your body straight, head up, arms to your sides, and hands pressed against thighs. Should you be wearing billowing clothes or a lifejacket, keep your hands tight against your chest and elbows pressed in firmly.

To raise yourself up again, push off from the bottom and raise your arms above your head.

Use a "split" or "stride" jump (**b**) for shallow water or to prevent yourself going in too deep. Start from a run or from a standing position and leap off from one foot. Keep the running pose in the air, legs spread forward and backward, not sideways, and enter the water in this position. Once the water reaches your waist, sweep your arms down to your sides and close your legs sharply. This acts as a brake and brings you to the surface quickly.

An alternative way to prevent injury is to enter the water in a tucked position (**c**), knees drawn up well against the chest, and arms around the front of the legs. Feet and rear strike the water first to make a large but painless splash.

submerging

Once in the water it may be necessary to swim under obstacles such as debris or burning oil. This can be done either headfirst (d) or feetfirst (e). If you have enough room, submerge headfirst. Bend at the hips, pushing your body, head, and arms down under the water. This is most easily done by using a quick breaststroke action with the arms. Then raise your legs into the air so that your body is driven well under the surface. Use a breaststroke arm action again to go deeper. Feetfirst submersion is done best from a vertical position. Push yourself up with a kick so that your body and arms are raised as far out of the water as possible. Their unsupported weight will then force you well under the surface. Keep your legs together, toes pointed downward. Once under the surface you can go deeper by sweeping your arms outward and upward from the thighs to finish above your head.

headfirst entry

In an emergency use a headfirst entry (f) only if you are an experienced swimmer, if the water is clear of obstructions, and if you know the depth of the water.

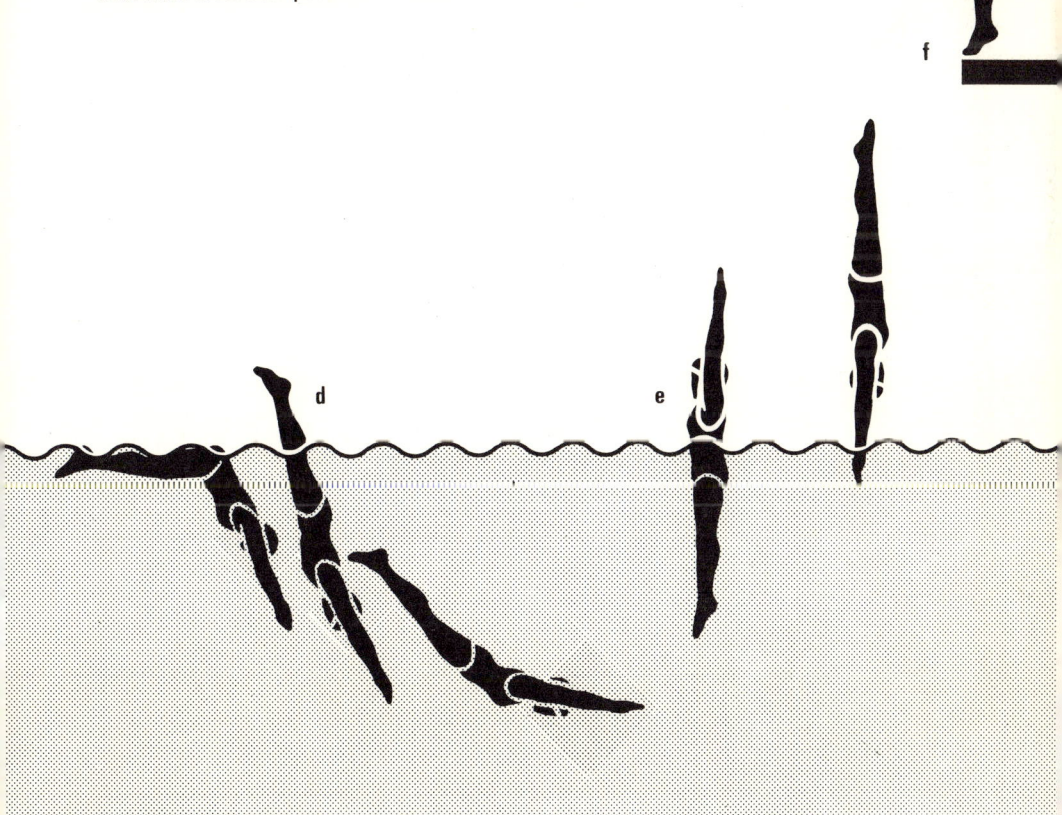

Helping yourself

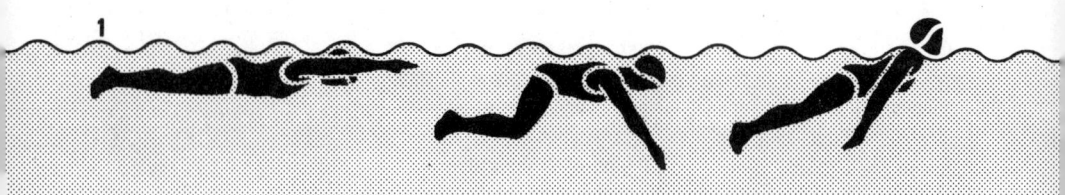

floating

With a few rare exceptions, anyone can float. And if you have to spend a long time in the water waiting for rescue, floating can save your life. Whether you float vertically (which is safest) or horizontally, the thing to remember is to let the water support you and to conserve energy by making as few movements as possible.

drownproofing (above)

Drownproofing is a survival technique designed for good, bad, and marginal floaters. It allows an exhausted swimmer to save energy and to stay afloat for hours on end.

1 If you are a nonfloater you need to keep moving. Stretch out flat, face down and arms over your head. Move your arms sideways and down to move forward. Drop your legs and kick. Raise your head, sweep your arms down and breathe out. Breathe in and put your face back in the water. Repeat the cycle.

2 If you float well you can rest in a vertical position, face submerged, arms and legs hanging limply. When you want to breathe, raise your arms and spread your legs. Bring your arms down and kick. Breathe out just before you reach the surface. Breathe in as you rise above the surface.

3 If you are a marginal floater rest with your back at a 45° angle. When you want to breathe stretch your arms in front of you, wrists crossed, palms outward. Open your legs ready to kick. Raise your head and begin to breathe out. Breathe in once your chin reaches the surface. You can stay on the surface by kicking gently and bringing your arms down.

clothing (below)
In water, clothing can be either a help or a hindrance. Widemesh or woolen clothes must be removed. Once these are waterlogged they become dangerous. But some clothes can be very useful either as insulators or inflated with air to make impromptu floats. Pants are ideal for this. Once removed each leg should be knotted. Air must then be forced in through the remaining opening. To get air in, tread water, hold the waistband, and sweep the pants through the air so that air is forced into the legs (**1**). Pull the open end into the water so that the air is trapped. An alternative is to hold the opening under the surface and either splash air in or plunge it in with a free hand (**2**). Even more simply you can duck below the pants and blow air upward into the opening (**3**). Once inflated, the pant legs can be tied together and pulled over the head so that the waistband sits on one's stomach rather like a lifejacket (**4**, **5**). Other clothes—blouses, shirts, dresses—can be inflated in much the same way. Skirts are more effective if they are kept on. Use the hem to scoop in air, and hold it down so that the air is trapped (**6**).

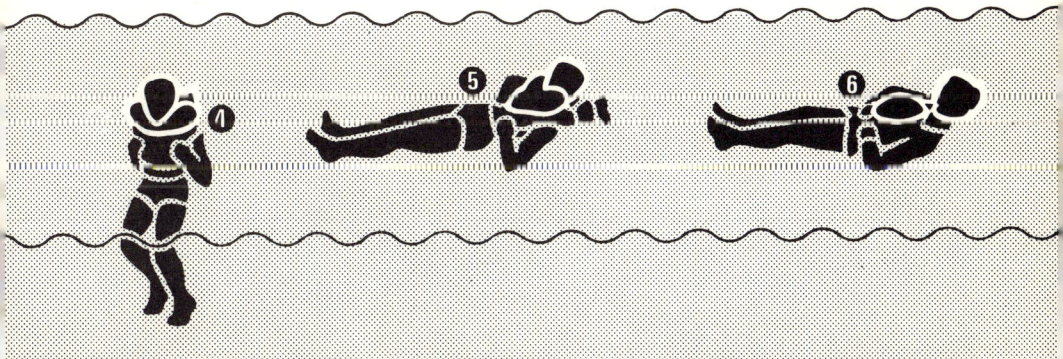

Helping others

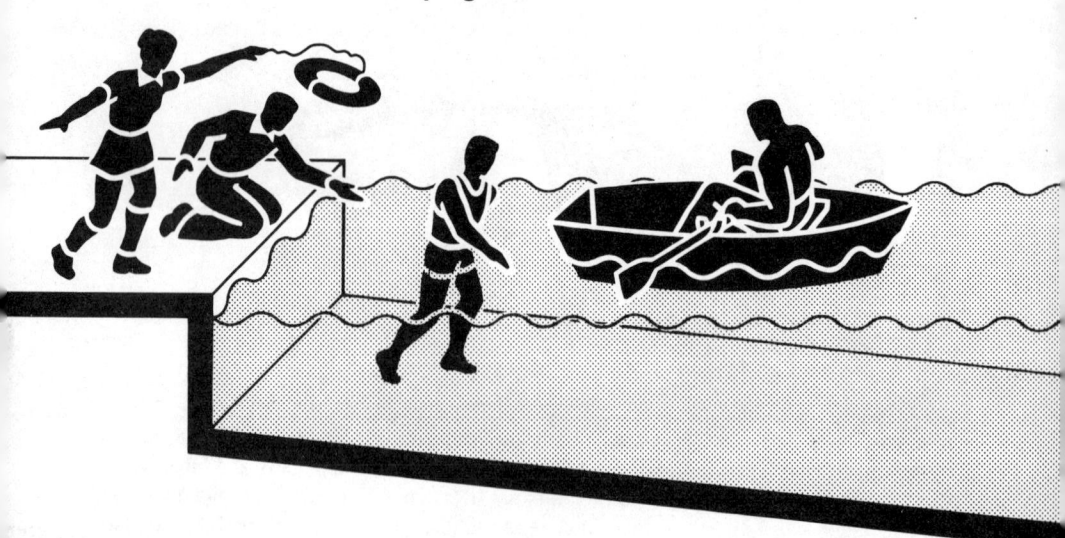

helping others
If you swim it is always worth bearing in mind what you would do in an emergency. Some day you might have to help a swimmer in difficulties and your action could save a life. Whenever you go swimming make a mental note of whatever safety equipment or rescue aids are available. Cold, exhaustion, and cramp are among the main causes of accidents but panic can be even more dangerous and can waste precious time. Even if you are not trained you can give help. Many accidents happen near land and most rescues are actually accomplished from land, either by reaching out to someone or by throwing something such as a rope. Even a nonswimmer can wade in a short distance and drag someone back to land. But swim out to someone only if you are certain you can bring him and yourself back safely.

course of action (above)
In an emergency there are six possible courses of action—reaching, throwing, wading, rowing, swimming, and towing. The first four are almost always preferable; swim out only as a last resort and ideally only if you are trained in rescue work. If you reach out for someone, keep yourself well braced to avoid being pulled in. If you throw out a support, aim for a spot just in front of the person in trouble.

approach (below)
If you swim out it is safest to approach a drowning person from the rear to avoid him clutching you in a panic. At the same time the person needs reassurance. If possible, circle him before getting in too close. This will give you a chance both to offer reassurance and to size up the situation.

panic holds (above)
You must free yourself immediately from a person who panics.
1 If your wrist or arm is grabbed by both hands of the panicky swimmer pull down and outward with the gripped arm, then slide past his shoulder and rise above him swinging your free arm around the back of his neck and grip his chin. Tow to safety.
2 If you are grabbed by the neck and head, tuck your chin into his shoulder and push upward on the other person's elbows, upper arms, or under the armpits.
towing (below)
The way in which you tow someone back to safety depends largely on his condition.
Use a cross-chest tow (**a**) with a nonswimmer. Place your arm across the person's chest, fingers tucked into his armpit. Swim sidestroke.
A tired but conscious person can rest his feet on your shoulders (**b**), allowing you to swim breaststroke while he floats.
Use an extended tow (**c**) for an unconscious or cooperative person. Hold the person's chin with one hand and tow him with your arm extended.
A chin tow (**d**) is used on a person needing firm control. Hold the victim's chin with one hand and clamp elbow of same arm onto his shoulder; swim in a cheek-to-cheek position with free arm.
If retrieving from under water (**e**), cradle his head on your arm and fin to the surface.

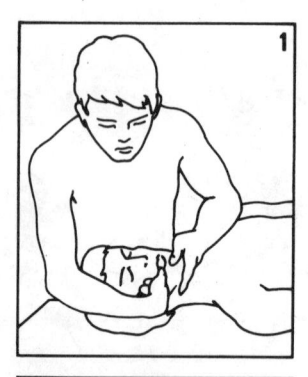

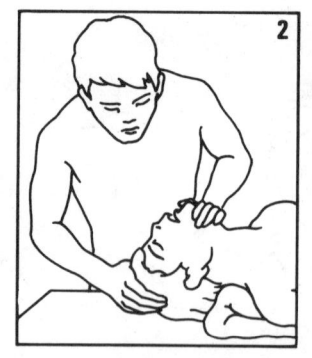

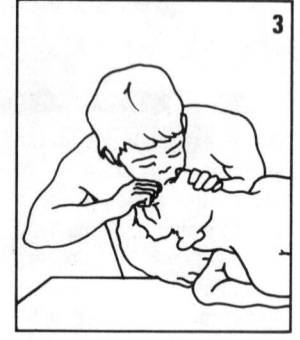

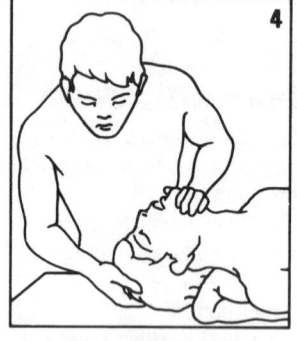

Helping others

mouth-to-mouth respiration

1 Turn the victim's head to one side and clear the mouth of any blockage.
2 Put a folded coat under the victim's shoulders and tilt his head right back.
3 Take a deep breath, cover the victim's mouth with yours, and, holding his nostrils closed, blow hard into his mouth so that his chest rises. For a small child cover nose and mouth with your mouth.
4 Remove your mouth and listen for the victim to breathe out. Repeat the blowing in at a rate of 10 a minute for an adult and 20 a minute for a child. Continue until the victim begins to breathe again.

landing

To get a person out of deep water push one of his arms onto the bank, boat, or landing-stage right up to the armpit. Holding that arm in position, get out yourself (**1**). Once on land, shift your grip (**2**), bounce the victim up and down for impetus (**3**), and drag him out (**4**). Always keep the victim's head above water.

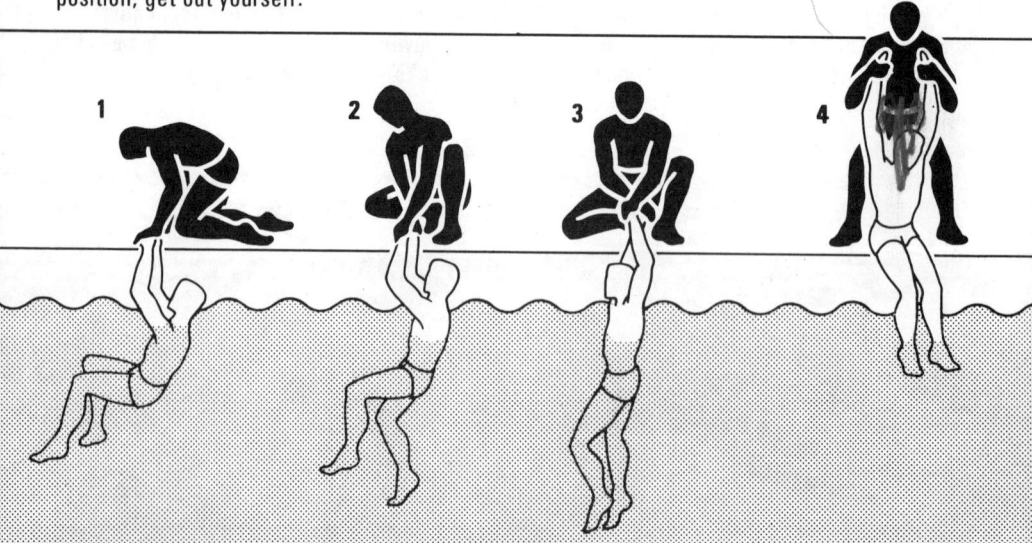

in-water aid
In a grave emergency start mouth-to-nose respiration in the water. Float at a right angle to the victim and support his trunk between shoulder blades or under far armpit with one hand. Close victim's mouth and support his jaw with your other hand while blowing hard into his nostrils. Continue to blow in once every five seconds.

shallow landing
To get an unconscious person onto land you need to be only waist-high in water. Float the victim onto his back, supporting him either with your hands or by placing one hand under his hips. Place one hand between his thighs and under his hips and grasp his near wrist with your free hand (**1**). Duck your head into the space between his near arm and side, and roll the victim over your shoulder. Before getting out of the water, switch your grasp on the wrist from your nearest hand to the hand that was between the victim's thighs so that you are holding him in a fireman's lift (**2**).

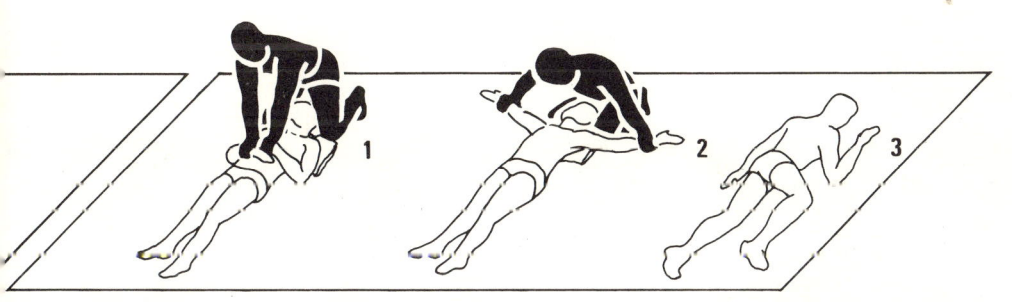

Silvester Brosch method
1 Lay victim on his back and put something under his shoulders to raise them and allow his head to fall back. Kneel at victim's head, grasping his arms at the wrists; then cross them and press firmly over lower chest forcing air out of his lungs.
2 Pull arms out and upward above victim's head. This will draw air into his lungs. Repeat this cycle about 12 times per minute until breathing starts again. Check mouth frequently for obstructions. To avoid victim inhaling vomit, mucus, or blood, keep victim's head extended and a little lower than the trunk.
3 Once the person is breathing again place him in the recovery position, head turned to one side so that he cannot choke.

Water fun

117

Water fun

Fun in the water can be fun for all. Once you can swim reasonably well there are endless games and activities you can enjoy either in the swimming pool or in the sea. In fact, you don't necessarily need to know how to swim at all to enjoy splashing about in the shallow end of the swimming pool.

In the following chapter you will find activities for both sea and pool. You can try some of the tricks and stunts by yourself or with a group, or you can have fun in the sea, body surfing or using a board. All these activities help to boost your confidence in the water and improve your swimming technique.

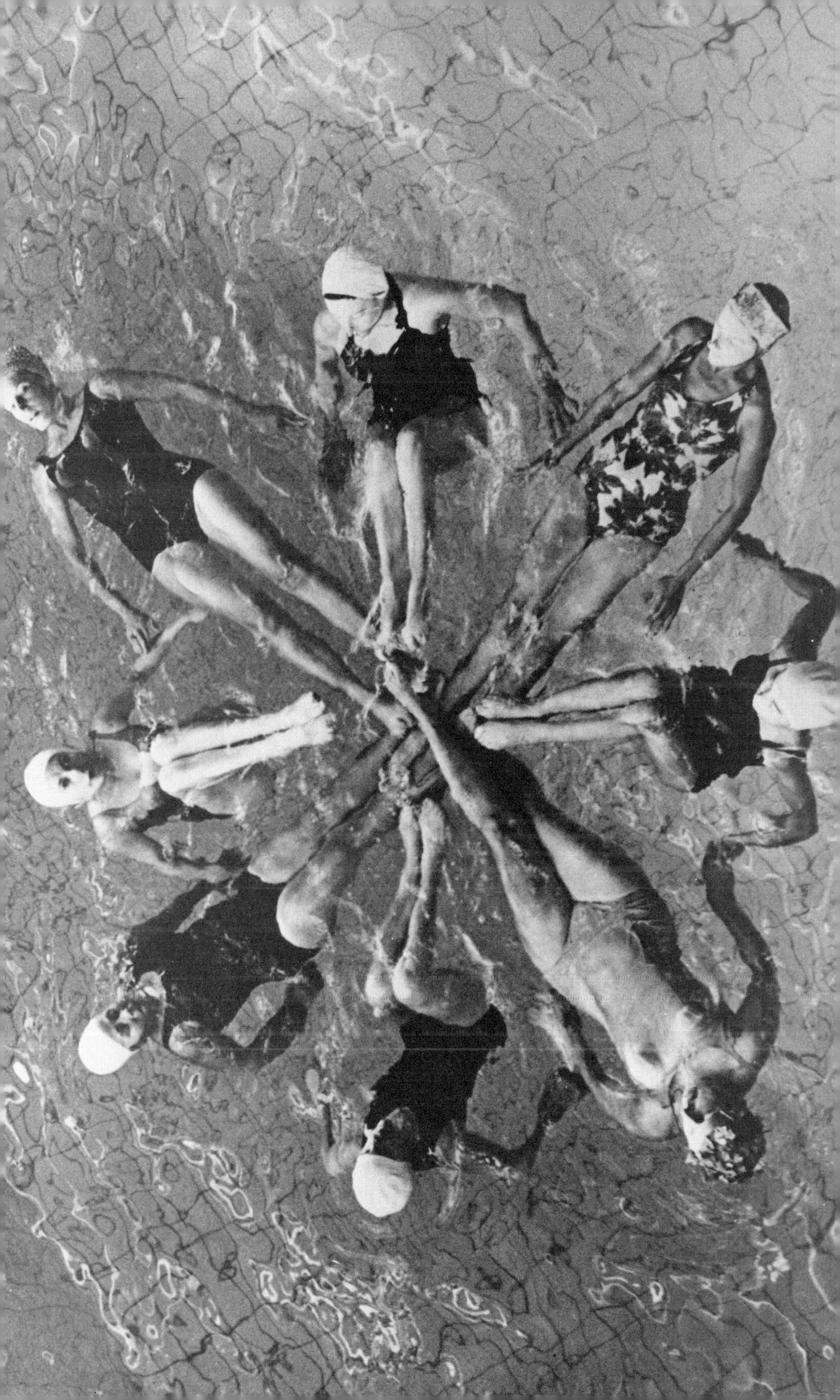

Fun and games

Once you can swim and are at home in the water there is no end to the water stunts you can do for interest and amusement. On this page we show some of the most common stunts. They are not difficult and you can try them on your own or with friends.

1 Make a ship by sculling with the hands only, leg raised for the funnel.
2 Somersault by ducking your head and pulling down and back with both hands.
3 Arms outstretched, roll your body over and over.
4 Try an underwater torpedo by pushing off under the water, spiraling your body until you break the surface.
5 Copy your partner's movements in a water version of "Simon Says".
6 The Dolphin or Porpoise is a combined breaststroke and shallow surface dive.
7 Try leapfrogging over your partner.
8 Make two teams of horse and rider, then try to unseat the other rider.

Surfing

Surfing has existed in the South Seas for hundreds of years and was observed by the explorer James Cook. In the early 1900s surfboards were heavy cumbersome objects but today, with the use of synthetic materials, boards are light and easy to handle and the sport can be enjoyed by men, women, and children. But surfing need not be limited to those with a board. Body surfing, where the body is used instead of a board, is popular and very exciting.

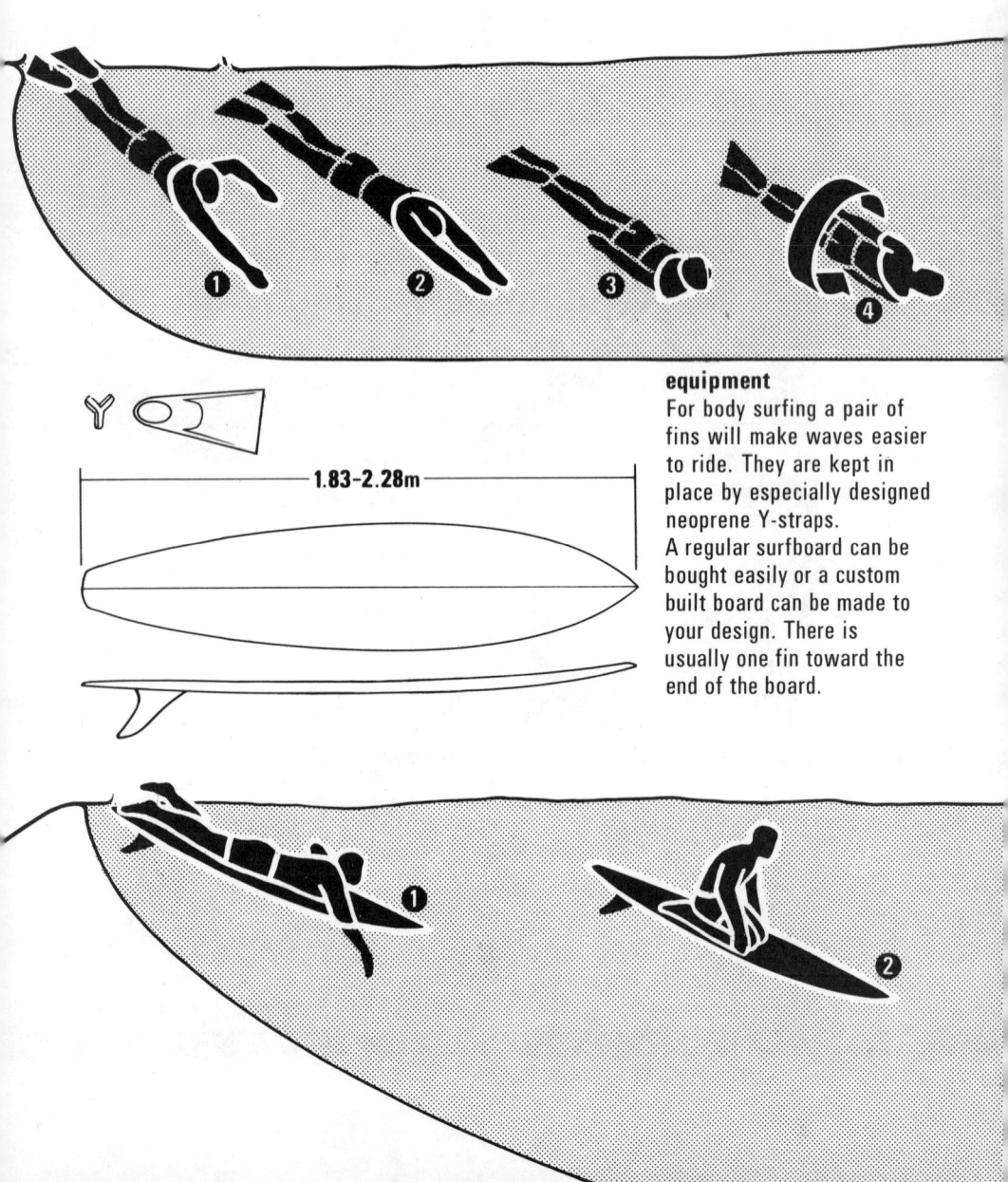

1.83-2.28m

equipment
For body surfing a pair of fins will make waves easier to ride. They are kept in place by especially designed neoprene Y-straps.
A regular surfboard can be bought easily or a custom built board can be made to your design. There is usually one fin toward the end of the board.

body surfing
1 Swim at a fast crawl until a wave lifts you;
2 once on the wave, drop head to bring weight forward, arms and hands pointing in front;
3 bring arms back to your sides, palms up or down; lift head

You can ride a wave in different ways:
4 try a "corkscrew" by dropping one shoulder and raising the opposite hip to revolve the body through the water;
5 by doing a half corkscrew you can surf on your back;
6 bring your arms in front;
lock your hands palms down and press down onto the water; raise your body so you are surfing on your hands;
7 when the wave gets too critical, do a forward roll pullout. Swim under the wave and back to the break.

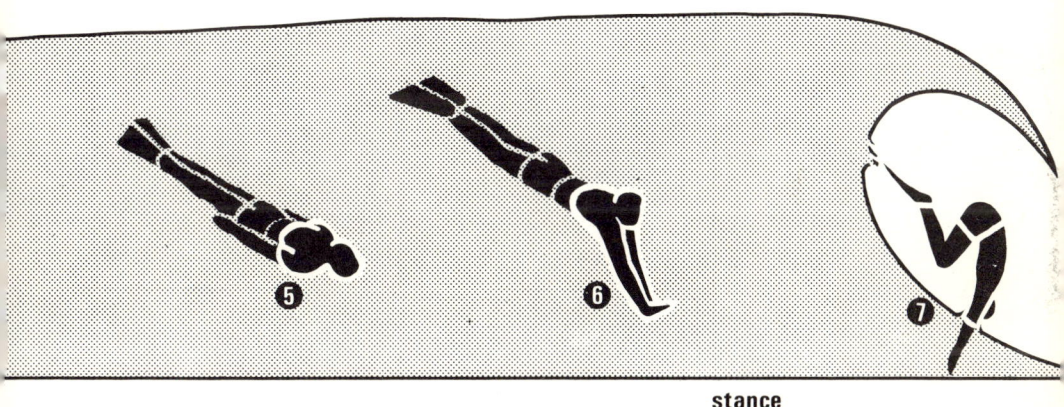

stance
When you stand up on the board your feet will naturally find a comfortable position. The usual stance is left foot leading (**a**). Right foot leading is known as a "goofy foot" stance (**b**).

board surfing
1 Paddle board until you feel the wave lift you;
2 grab the rails or edges of the board and pull up to a kneeling position;
3 once you can catch a wave without "pearling" (nose diving) or stalling, stand up on the board with knees bent. Use your arms to keep your balance. If you fall, try to fall over the back or side of the board.

Surfing

1 Take off toward peak power source;

2 stand up; throw weight forward toward outside edge; top turn to start rhythm;

3 turn left after top turn and aim for the bottom of the wave; throw your weight forward and down, with the emphasis on the inside edge;

4 as you reach the trough of the wave and maximum speed, hit the turn; if you turn too early you will lose potential speed; if you turn too late you lose the speed gained in the drop;

5 when the edge of the board is buried in the wave, aim for the upper corner; keep your weight forward;

6 on the way up the face of the wave, release off your inside edge; go to the outside edge and aim back down the face for more power.

Surfing

nose ride
This is good fun but also functional. When the board is trimmed or planing properly, put your weight forward and walk as close to the nose as possible. Curl a foot over the nose to "hang five"; then try "hanging ten" with both feet over the nose.

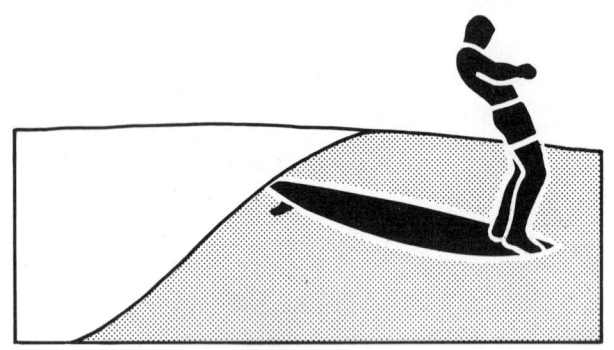

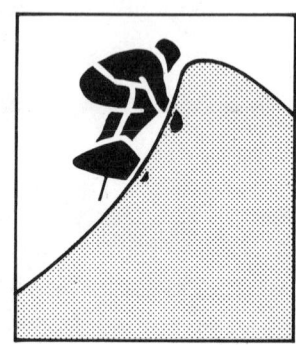

side slip
This is a controlled fall. The fin breaks loose leaving only the rail in contact with the wave. This stalls the board, allowing the wave to catch up with you.

tube ride
This is surfing's ultimate thrill. It can be done only in large forward-throwing waves that break on rock bottoms. Take a bottom run, then stall the board. The wave will loop over you as you crouch beneath.

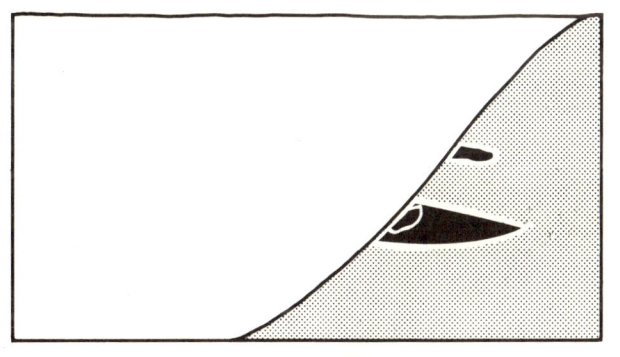

cut back
When you have gone too far out onto the shoulder and you are losing power, turn back into the power source. Timing is of the essence, as with all surfing maneuvers.

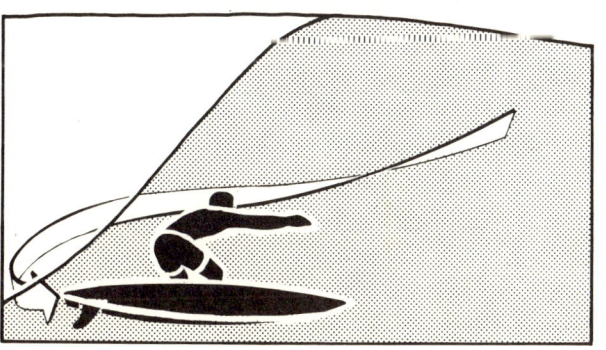

Windsurfing

Windsurfing is the latest water sport. It combines surfing and sailing into an art that can be quickly learned. Although the windsurfer is basically a surfboard with a mast and sail, it is not the strength of the wave that carries the board forward, but the strength of the wind. The windsurfer is designed for sailing singlehanded. To start with, practice with someone who has already gained control over his board. The safety factor is obviously higher when sailing in pairs or in a group.

sailing at speed

Good balance, grip, and fast reactions are needed to keep a smooth flow when sailing at top speeds. The front foot is braced against the mast with the back foot on the outer edge of the board. The knees are bent so that your center of gravity is over the middle of the board.

As the wind eases, get momentary counterpressure from the sail by pulling the boom back over the board. If you feel yourself falling, always fall off the board backward to avoid falling onto the daggerboard or fin.

129

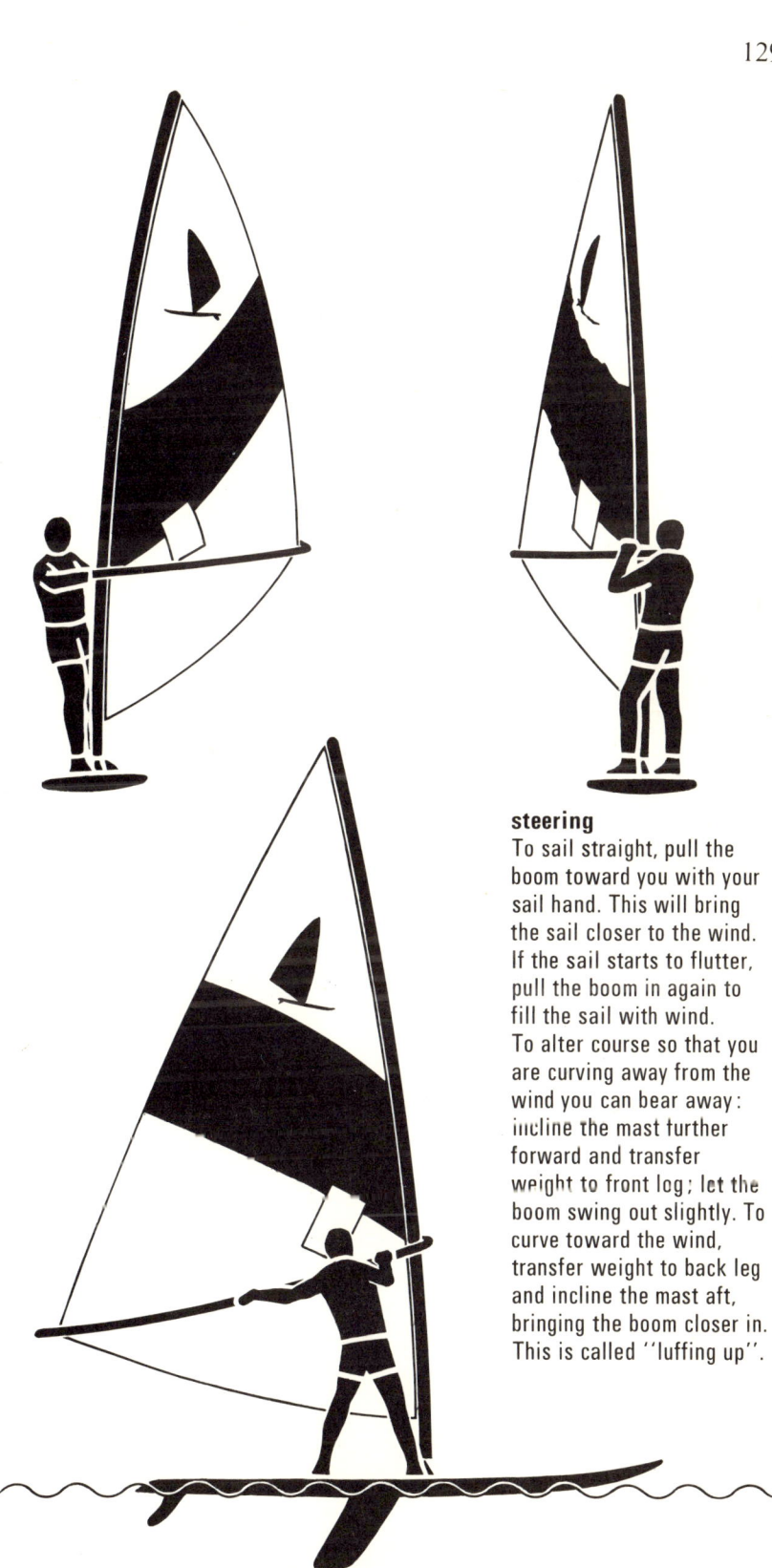

steering
To sail straight, pull the boom toward you with your sail hand. This will bring the sail closer to the wind. If the sail starts to flutter, pull the boom in again to fill the sail with wind.
To alter course so that you are curving away from the wind you can bear away: incline the mast further forward and transfer weight to front leg; let the boom swing out slightly. To curve toward the wind, transfer weight to back leg and incline the mast aft, bringing the boom closer in. This is called "luffing up".

Water skiing

Water skiing is no longer only the privilege of those living around the Mediterranean. It is an exciting and exhilarating sport and is now being tried by people everywhere. You need a power boat that is easily maneuvered and has good all-round visibility, water skis, and a tow rope with a handle. Skis are usually made of varnished wood, about 1.7m (5ft 6in) long, and the tow rope should be about 21m (70ft) long.

Probably the hardest part of water skiing is getting started. The deep-water start is the most usual and once you have mastered this you can set off from anywhere. Grasp the tow rope and lean slightly back with your head forward, knees bent under your body, and ski tips protruding above the surface. The boat moves away slowly, and as the slack of the tow rope is taken up so you move from crouching into an upright position. Keep your arms straight and head up and don't let the boat pull you forward; counteract its pull with your back and leg muscles. Everyone falls at some time or other. When you fall, remember to let go of the tow rope immediately. Tuck your head in and bring your knees up to your chest so that you roll into a ball. Fall backward if at all possible.

Once you have mastered the basics of water skiing you have almost limitless scope. You can try display skiing or you can water ski with a partner. Or you can move on to mono skiing. For this you use one ski only and it is the fastest aspect of water skiing. The advantage of using only one ski is that it allows you to bank and turn sharply crossing the wake of the boat.

Ornamental swimming

Synchronized or ornamental swimming is rather like formation dancing in the water and can be great fun when done by a group of people. Whether swimming or floating you can make many interesting designs or patterns. And to make your patterns larger, just add more people. This type of water display was popularized in the United States, where national championships have been held since 1945.

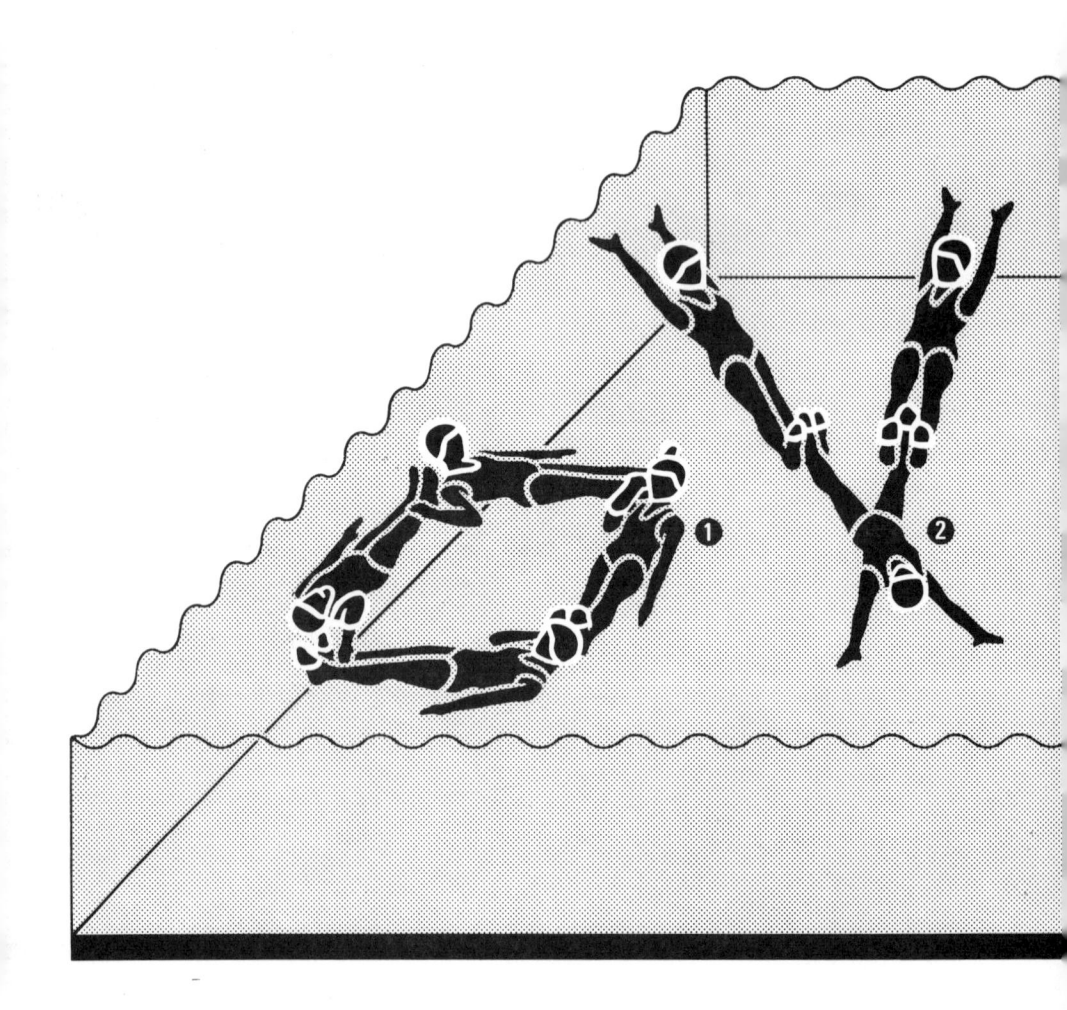

1 A floating square is made up of four people at right angles to each other, head to feet. Each person grips another's ankle on the inside of the square;

2 The scissor float is made by one person floating in an X-shape. Two others float, pointing in the opposite direction, arms stretched out, feet interlocking with the first person.

3 With massed floating, attractive doily patterns can be made. Start with a square of people in the X-position. More people join on, gripping each other's hands and feet.

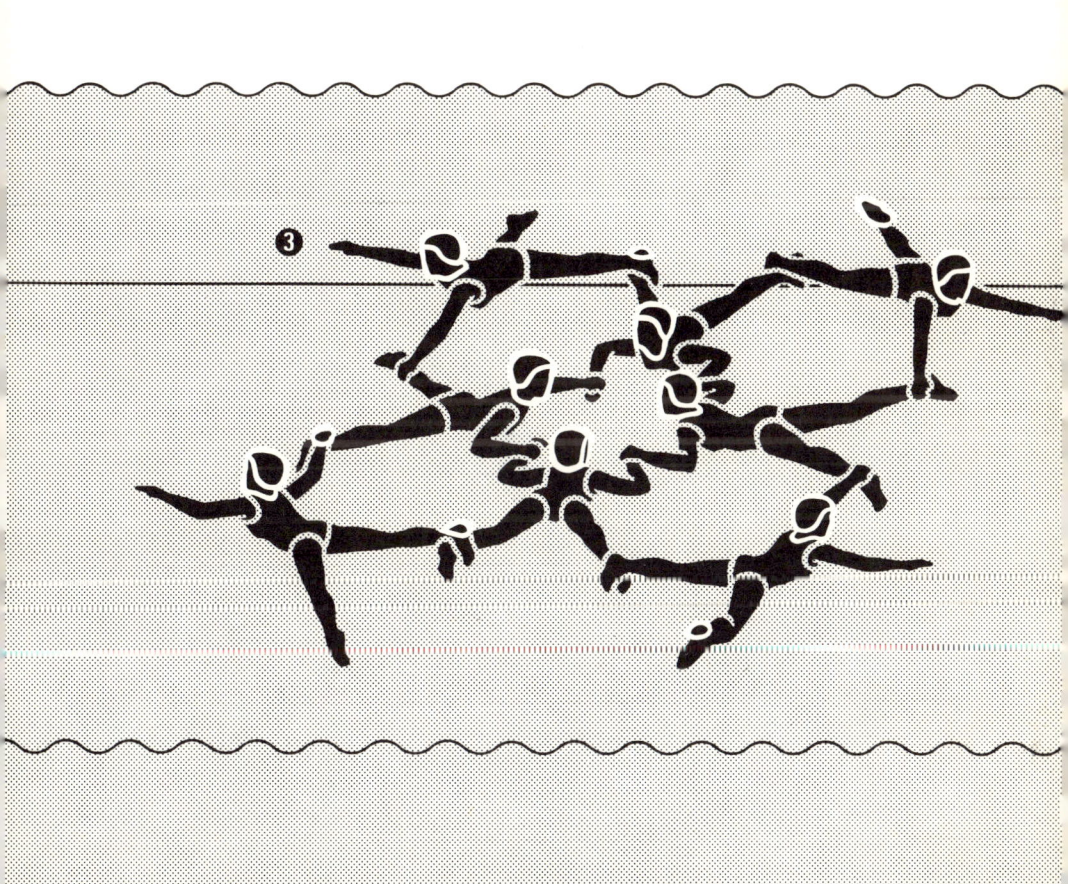

Water polo

Water polo was once seen as a cross between unarmed combat and underwater soccer. Today it is considered to be one of the fastest, most skilled, and most exhilarating of team games. It is a demanding game, requiring a high standard of swimming and expert ball handling. At the same time it is an exciting game and an excellent way to learn teamwork and team tactics.

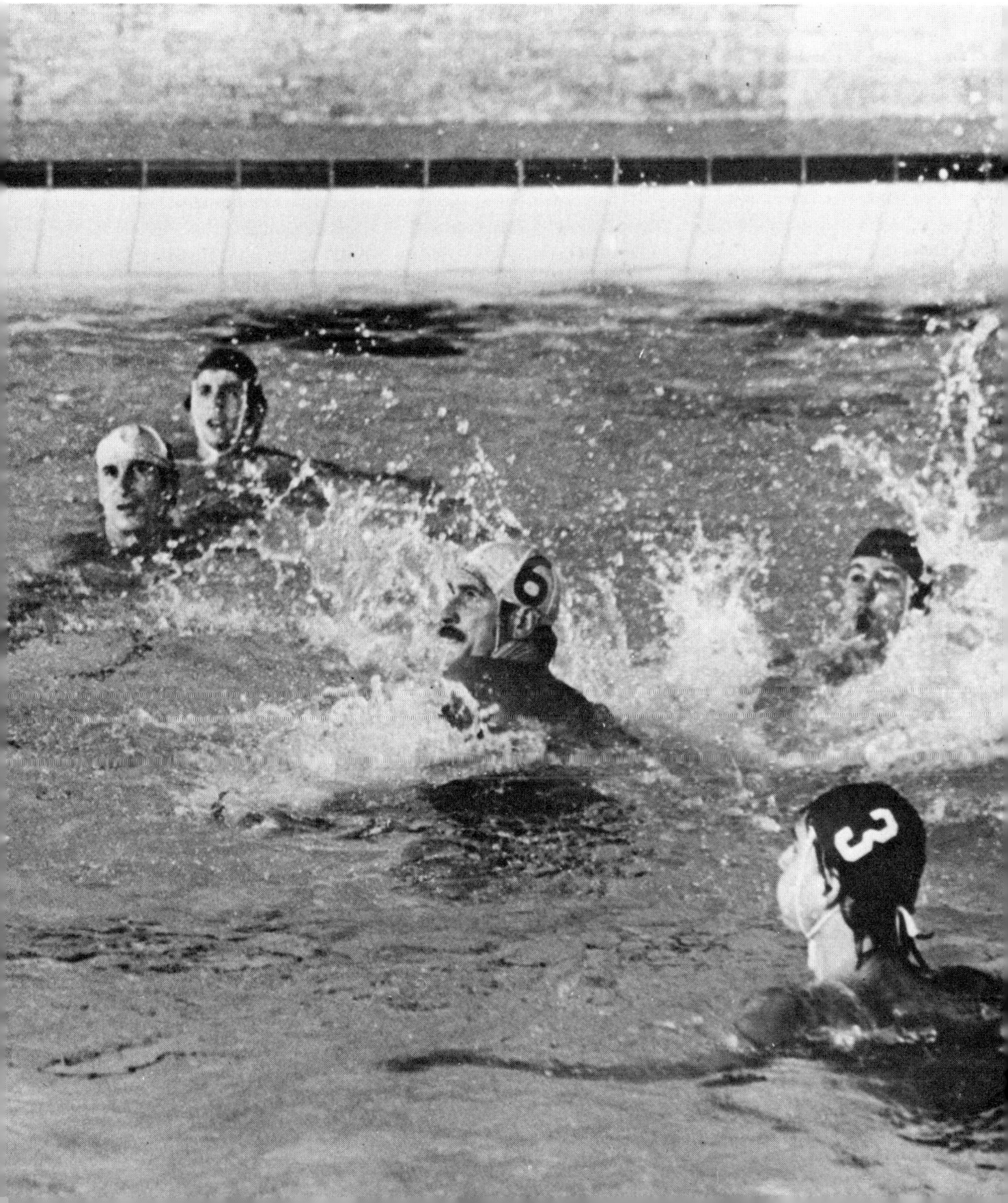

Rules

Water polo is a team game played by two teams of up to 11 a side, only seven of whom may be in the water at the same time. The ball may be propelled one-handed, but not punched by any player other than the goalkeeper. Each team attempts to score by putting the ball into its opponents' goal.

officials

The game is controlled by up to seven officials: two referees, two goal judges, timekeepers, and secretaries. The referee uses a whistle and two flags (one blue, one white). He stops and starts the game, and decides fouls, goals, and throws. He applies the advantage rule by which fouls are not declared if the offending team would benefit, and can also order any player out of the water for a 'major foul'. The two goal judges each have a white flag to signal goal throws and a red flag to signal corner throws. They sit opposite the referee at each end of the pool and level with the goal line. The timekeepers use stopwatches to record playing time and a whistle to indicate the end of a period.
Secretaries record major fouls and signal with a red flag when any player is awarded a third personal fault. They also control periods of exclusion, signalling when a player may reenter the game.

playing area

Maximum dimensions are illustrated; minimum dimensions are 20m long by 8m wide.
The minimum depth is 1m, or 1.80m in Olympic, world championship, and international competitions. All lines must be visible throughout the game; suggested colors are:
goal line and half-distance line, white;
2m line, red;
4m line, yellow.
There must be sufficient room for the referee to walk along the edge of the pool.

teams and dress

A team comprises 11 players, of whom four are substitutes. All players wear trunks and numbered caps. One team wears white caps, the other blue. The goalkeeper's cap is red. Club colors may be worn in some competitions. A player losing his cap must replace it at the next stoppage. No player may oil or grease his body.

30 m

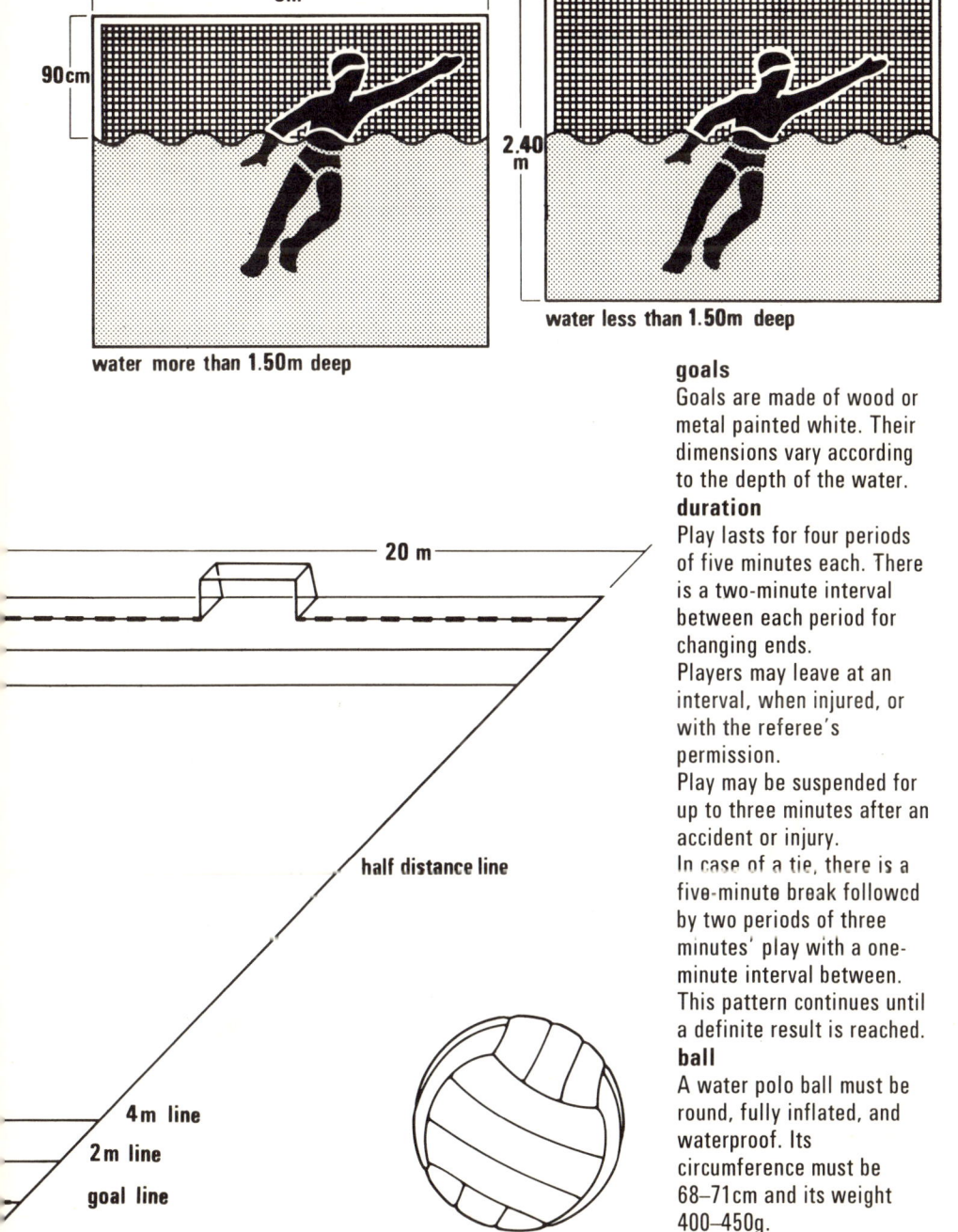

goals
Goals are made of wood or metal painted white. Their dimensions vary according to the depth of the water.

duration
Play lasts for four periods of five minutes each. There is a two-minute interval between each period for changing ends.
Players may leave at an interval, when injured, or with the referee's permission.
Play may be suspended for up to three minutes after an accident or injury.
In case of a tie, there is a five-minute break followed by two periods of three minutes' play with a one-minute interval between. This pattern continues until a definite result is reached.

ball
A water polo ball must be round, fully inflated, and waterproof. Its circumference must be 68–71cm and its weight 400–450g.

Basic skills

strokes used (above)
Speed and stamina are the secrets of success in water polo. The strokes most frequently used are breaststroke (**a**) for readiness, back crawl (**b**) for evasive action or taking a shot, and front crawl (**c**) for speed. Visibility is vital at all times so a player's face must never be in the water. For the front crawl this means using a deeper kick than normal. Outfield players, who are not allowed to stand on the bottom of the pool, need to know how to tread water. There are two ways of doing this. In the first (**d**) a type of breaststroke leg kick is used. It has a short kick and the feet do not finish together or touch the player's seat. In the second method (**e**) an "eggbeater" kick is used. The player kicks his legs alternately in a scissors-like motion. It is very effective and particularly useful for goalkeepers.

picking up the ball (below)
There are three main ways of getting the ball out of the water. The simplest way is to place a hand under the ball and to lift or scoop it up. In the second method—the "rolling pickup"—the player places his hand on top of the ball, rolls it sideways and downward, and lifts it out. By the third method the player pushes the ball down sharply so that it bounces out. As it bounces, the player's hand moves underneath.

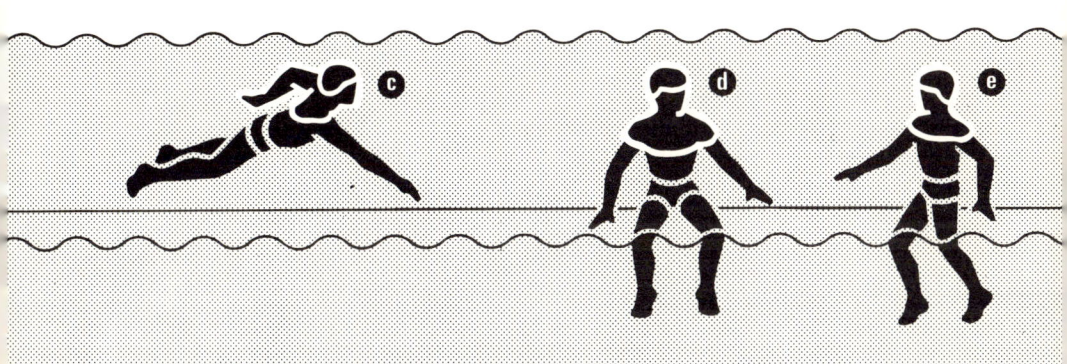

throwing and catching (below)

Water obstructs movement, so it is much harder to throw a ball accurately in water than on land. It needs a lot of practice. This is best done first in shallow rather than deep water. To throw the ball the arm needs to be held almost straight behind the shoulder. With the arm clear of the water, the ball should be thrown overarm with a flick of the wrist so that the fingers follow the ball through. Look directly at the target for the entire throw. In deep water give a sharp kick to raise the upper body out of the water. When catching, the catching arm should be kept well forward in front of the body. Once the ball is caught, the arm should move back over the shoulder with it, ready for another throw.

holding the ball (below)

The ball should be held in the palm of the hand, fingers and thumb outstretched to give maximum control when throwing.

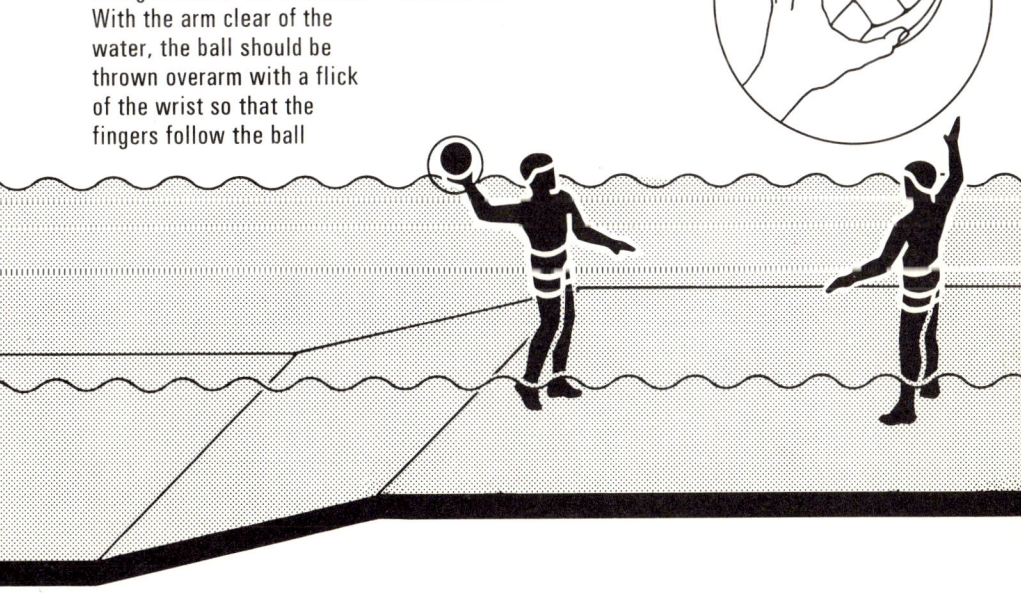

Basic skills

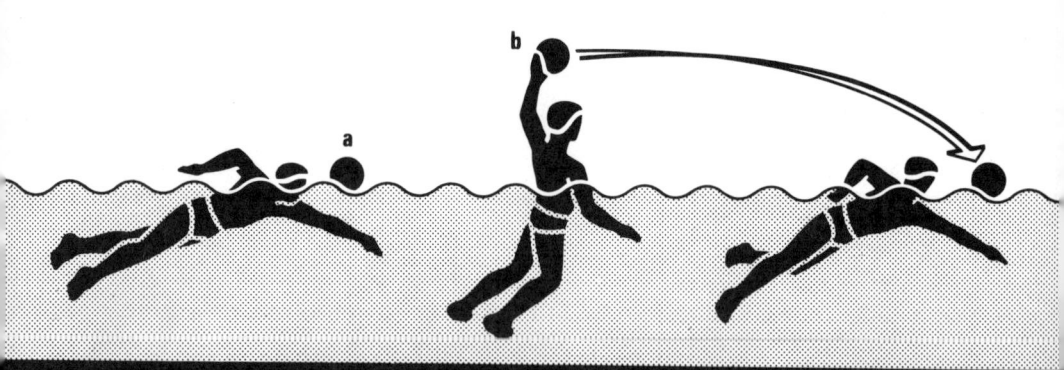

dribbling and passing
(above)

It is important to get into a good position before trying to pass the ball. You dribble the ball until you are in the right position for passing, then lower your legs, raise your arm high, and throw the ball over the arms of your opponents. Dribbling (**a**) is quite skilled. The front crawl is used and the ball is carried forward by the small wave created in front of the face. But to begin with, you may need to help the ball forward by tapping it with your forehead. Use your arms to keep the ball in position.

There are two basic types of pass—the wet pass (**b**) and the dry pass (**c**). In the first the ball is thrown to a moving player, just in front of his face, so that he can move forward and gain control of the ball without stopping. The dry pass is used to throw the ball to a stationary player. The receiving player raises a hand above his head, propels himself out of the water with an eggbeater kick and, as he catches the ball, leans back to avoid being tackled by an opponent.

marking and tackling
(below left)

Good defense relies on good marking and tackling. Normally you mark an opponent by placing yourself between him and your own goal. You may tackle only when an opponent handles the ball, not when he is dribbling. When tackling from behind (**a**), the opponent's throwing arm is grabbed to prevent him from either passing or shooting. In a forward tackle (**b**) the defensive player pushes his opponent down into the water with his right arm while raising his left arm to intercept the ball.

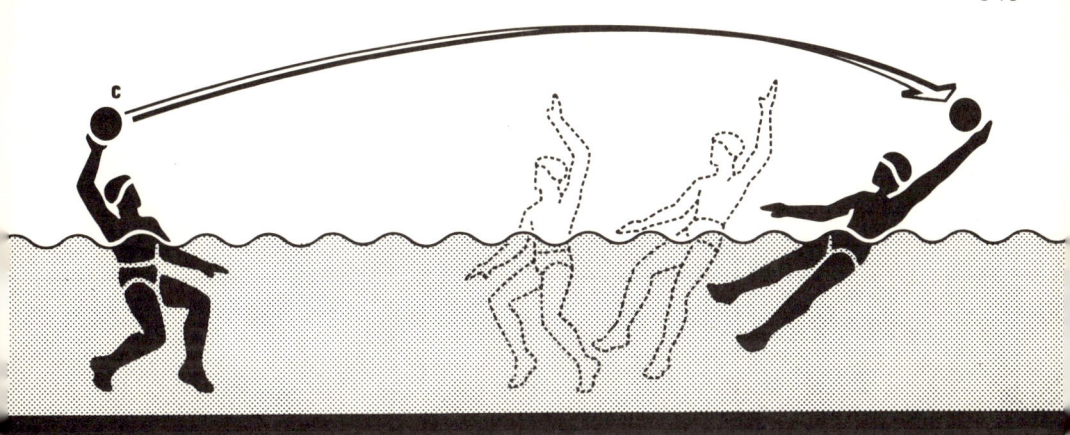

shooting (below)
Shooting is the most flamboyant aspect of water polo and the one that makes the headlines. Essentially the type of shot used depends on the situation—where opponents are placed, where the goalkeeper is, and how much time is available. Given that a player is fairly free of opponents, a lob shot (**a**) can be used. In this the shooter takes a vertical position and heaves the ball in a long, high arch over the arms of other players into an unguarded corner of the goal. For the element of surprise a backhand shot (**b**) is effective. A player with his back to the goal bypasses his opponent by quickly scooping up the ball and shooting it over his shoulder. The moving player with no time to adopt a vertical position should try for a push shot (**c**), gently pushing the ball toward the goal before shooting.

Goalkeeping

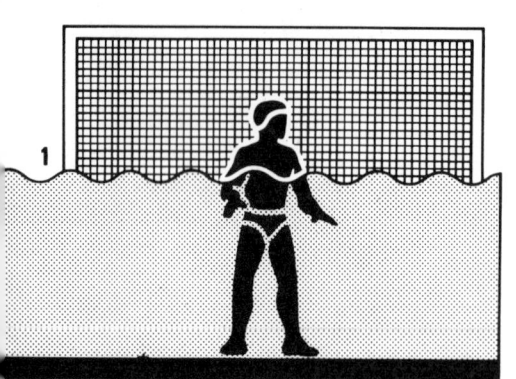

goalkeeping (above)
The goalkeeper's main job is defense. Within his 4m (13ft) area he enjoys certain privileges of which he should take maximum advantage. He is the only player who may (**1**) stand and walk on the bottom of the pool, (**2**) punch the ball with a clenched fist, (**3**) use both hands, and (**4**) jump from the floor of the pool. But there are also various things that the goalkeeper may not do. He must not cross the half-distance line, send the ball beyond the opponent's 4m (13ft) line, or hold the bar, rail, or trough at the end of the pool. A good goalkeeper needs to be agile, intelligent, and fast. Good defensive tactics include the ability to lunge well out of the water, good maneuverability, and the ability to position well in goal. At the same time the goalkeeper must be able to help his team's offensive efforts by passing accurately and quickly.

out of play (below)
The ball is out of play (**a**) when it hits the side of the pool and bounces back into the water (**1**), when it completely crosses the goal line (**2**), and when it is sent out of the side of the pool (**3**), or when it hits an overhead obstruction (**4**). A goal throw (**b**) is awarded for (2). This is taken by the defending goalkeeper from the goal line between the goal posts. In cases (1) and (3) free throws are awarded and the ball is returned to play by

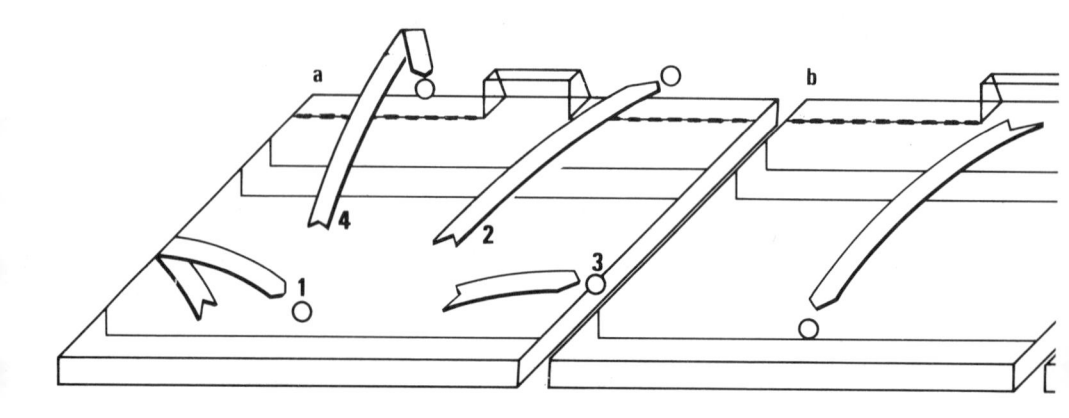

the opposing player nearest to where the ball went out. Corner throws (c) are awarded where a defender sends the ball over his own goal line. They must be taken by the attacking player nearest to where the ball went out and from the 2m (6ft 6in) mark on that side of the pool.

If the ball hits an overhead obstruction, the referee awards a neutral throw between two opposing players, directly between the obstruction.

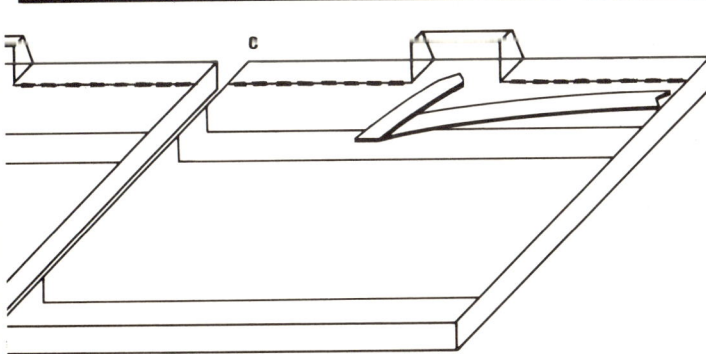

scoring (left)
It is not enough to be able to shoot a ball well; good aim is also essential. The basic rule-of-thumb is quite simple: aim for those spots in the goal that are the hardest for the goalkeeper to defend. In general these are the upper and lower corners of the goal and around the goalkeeper's head. A goal is scored when the ball has completely crossed the goal line between the posts and under the crossbar. At least two players must have touched the ball after a start or restart. The ball may be dribbled into the goal but not punched. Apart from using a clenched fist, a player can score with any part of his body.

Officials

officials

The number of officials varies depending on the type of competition. But in general there are one or two referees, two goal judges, timekeepers, and secretaries. The timekeepers and secretaries may have assistants if they need them. The referee (**1**) stands on the half-distance line. As near to him as possible, between him and the 4m line, are the timekeepers (**2**) and secretaries (**4**). The goal judges (**3**) are directly level with the goal line at either end of the pool.

the referee

The referee is the most important official and his decision is final. His equipment consists of a whistle, which he uses to stop the game, and two flags, one blue and one white, which are used for signaling.

flag positions

To indicate a penalty throw (**a**) the referee holds his flag in a vertical position high above his head. He then lowers the flag and at the same time blows his whistle. At the start of play and after a goal the referee holds his flag horizontally above his head (**b**), lowers it, and at the same time blows his whistle. For a free throw (**c**) the referee displays the flag showing the colors of the team awarded the throw. The same applies for a goal or corner throw except that for these he also points with his other hand toward the goal or corner.

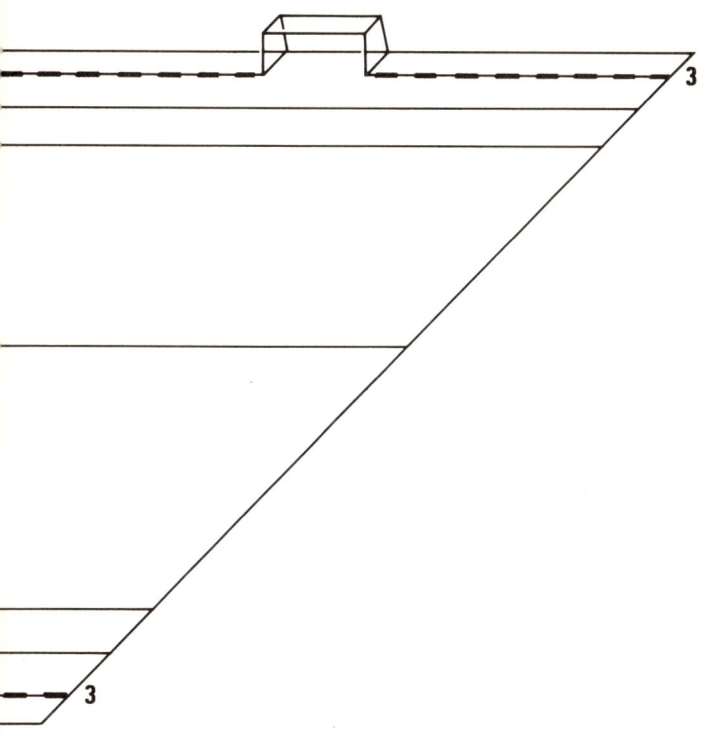

secretaries

The job of the secretaries is to record all major fouls, who commits them, and the time at which they happen. They use a red flag to signal a third personal fault. They also control the length of time a player is excluded and signal his reentry with a flag that is the same color as the excluded player's cap.

timekeepers

Timekeepers use whistles to indicate the end of a playing period, and stopwatches. Their job is to record actual playing time and intervals; to record the exclusion time of any player who has been sent out of the water; and to record how long the ball is held continuously by each team.

goal judges

Both goal judges have a white flag and a red flag. The white flag signals a goal throw; the red flag is used to signal a corner throw. Both flags are used to signal a goal. Each goal judge is responsible for keeping a correct record of goals scored at his end of the pool. At the start of each period, the goal judge displays the red flag to show that the players are correctly positioned on their goal line.

Fouls

fouls

There are a number of offenses that may occur during a game of water polo. They are classified as major fouls, which are penalized by personal faults and periods of exclusion, and ordinary fouls, which are penalized by a free throw.

Major fouls are the most serious. They range from acts of brutality to illegally preventing a goal from being scored within the 4m area (**1**). A player who commits a major fault is awarded a personal fault and ordered out of the water for a period of 45 seconds or until a goal is scored, whichever is the sooner. A penalty throw is taken by a member of the opposing team if a defending player commits a foul in the 4m area which, in the referee's opinion, prevented a goal. If a player collects three personal faults he is excluded from the rest of the game and a substitute may take his place.

1 No player, other than the goalkeeper inside his own 4m area, may use both hands to hit the ball.

2 No player, other than the goalkeeper inside his own 4m area, may stand, walk, or jump from the bottom of the pool.

3 It is an ordinary foul for any player to take or hold the ball under water when being tackled.

There are many ordinary fouls. They include assisting another player at the start of a period, interfering with a player who is not holding the ball, being within 2m (6ft 6in) of the opposing goal unless behind the ball, and holding onto or pushing off from the goal posts (**2**). Each team will commit many minor fouls during the course of the game. For example, nearly all players at some time unintentionally impede a player who is not holding the ball. When an ordinary foul occurs, the referee blows his whistle and raises a flag corresponding to the cap color of the team awarded the throw.

A free throw is then taken from where the foul was committed. The throw must be made in such a way that other players can see the ball leave the player's hand. The player taking the throw may either throw the ball or drop it into the water and dribble it before passing.

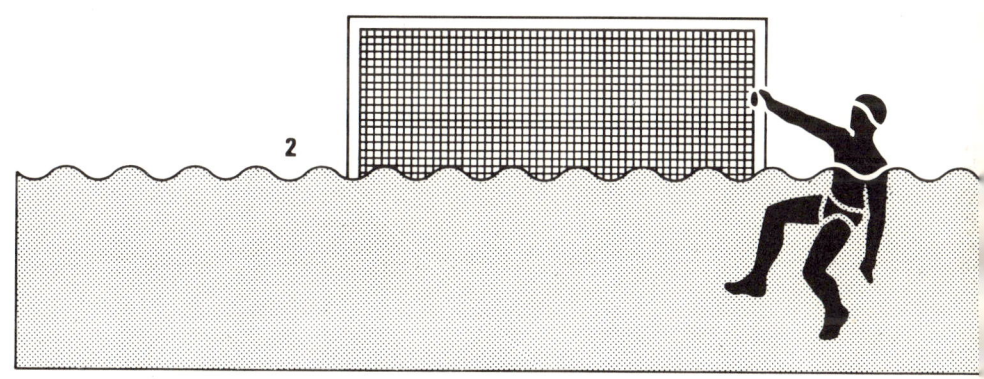

4 It is a major foul for any player to commit a brutal act such as kicking or striking an opponent.

5 It is a major offense to sink, hold back, or pull back an opponent who is not holding the ball.

6 It is an ordinary foul for a player to splash water in an opponent's face.

STA DISTANCE AWARD 800 METRES

20 OF THE 50 MILES
SWIM AND STAY FIT

Alfred W. Cantwell
NATIONAL DIRECTOR, SAFETY SERVICES

THE AMERICAN NATIONAL RED CROSS
This certifies that
Susan Marqusee
has completed the SENIOR course of instruction in
LIFESAVING AND WATER SAFETY
at Camp Regis - AppleJack

8/20/75

R. M. Oswald
National Director
Safety Programs

AMATEUR SWIMMING ASSOC — PERSONAL SURVIVAL — SILVER STANDARD

LONDON SCHOOLS SWIMMING ASSOCIATION

CERTIFICATE OF THE 1st CLASS GRANTED TO

Kate Greenacre

THIS 12th DAY OF Oct.r 1909

SIGNED *H. Bradbury*

HON: SEC:

NATIONAL WATER SKI ASSOCIATION

DATE 8-21-73

Training

In recent years there has been a tremendous improvement in the performance of swimmers. This is due partly to improved stroke techniques but also partly to the increased emphasis on training. Not everyone wants to be an Olympic competitor, but the exercises shown on this page will certainly help to improve your swimming technique as well as increasing your physical well-being.

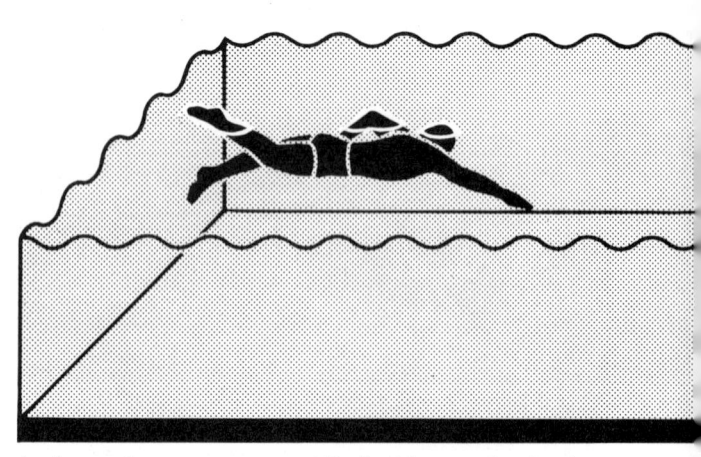

in the pool
Some of the top competitors spend at least two hours a day in the pool practicing their strokes and warming up. If you are thinking of entering any swimming contest you should also spend a certain amount of time daily in the pool. You can warm up by swimming between 360 and 720m (400 and 800yd) using any stroke. Then you should practice your arm and leg strokes separately. To do this try swimming for about 360m (400yd) with a small board between your ankles. This will force you to concentrate on improving your arm technique. To practice your kick, rest your hands on the board and swim for another 360m (400yd).

exercises

It is a good idea to have a regular workout either at home or in a gym. Don't start straight off with strenuous exercising but allow yourself a warming-up period first.

a Weight-lifting is ideal for improving strength and stamina;
b isometric exercises tighten up flabby muscles; and
c loosening-up exercises keep the body supple.

fitness

Fitness is always important not only for swimming but also for everyday living. Watch what you eat and how much; you cannot be fit if you overeat or live on starchy foods. Walk whenever possible instead of hopping into a car or onto a bus. Brisk walking burns off calories and also improves your circulation. Avoid overtiredness, which affects both mind and body; and try to get a good night's sleep every night.

When you have finished your training for the day, don't hang around dripping water, or you will get cold. Have a warm shower, dry off, and get dressed. If you want to stay by the side of the pool watching others, invest in a toweling jacket, preferably one with a hood. At the very least wrap a large towel around yourself.

Glossary and index

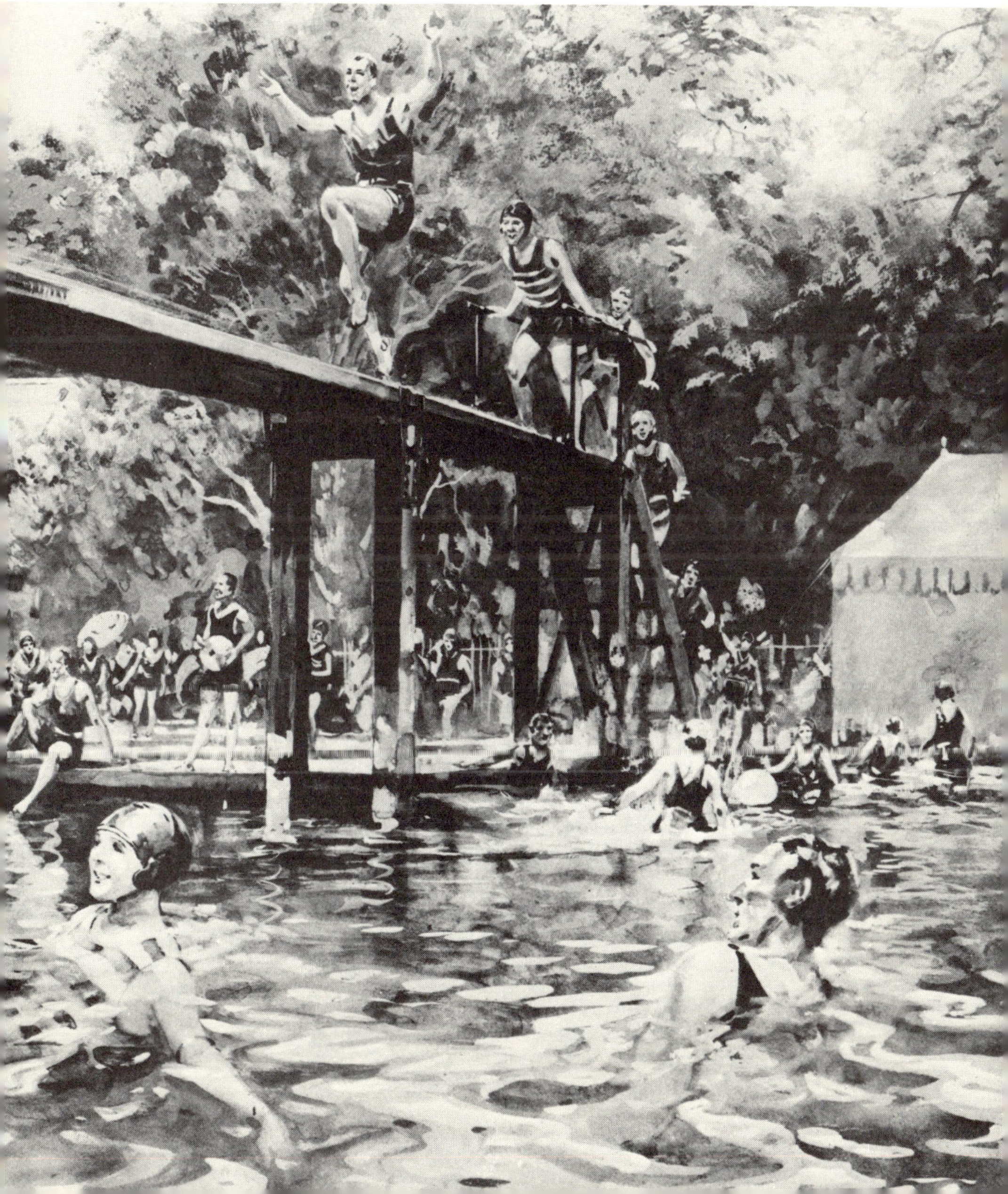

Glossary

anoxia — shortage of oxygen caused by hyperventilation; in underwater swimming it can be fatal.

approach — name given to the "run up" to the end of a diving board before takeoff; generally consists of three steps and a hurdle.

aqualung — popular name for self-contained underwater breathing apparatus (scuba) generally consisting of two air cylinders, a demand valve or regulator, and breathing tubes.

atmosphere — term used by divers to describe pressure of 14.7lbs per square inch; as a diver descends pressure increases by one atmosphere every 33 feet.

back dive — diver takes off facing the platform, back to the water, and continues backwards through the air.

bends — diver's paralysis, a serious condition which generally effects only deep-sea divers; it is caused by rising to the surface too quickly.

cork float — simple method of floating in which the body is rolled into a ball, hands clasping the knees, so that just the back breaks the surface. It gets its name from the way in which the body bobs on the surface like a cork.

corkscrew — surfing term used to describe the way in which a surfer revolves through the water.

cross-chest tow — method of towing a nonswimmer back to land; the rescuer holds the victim across the chest with his arm and swims sidestroke.

cross position — in diving, the position assumed at the highest point of the hurdle, legs straight, arms held horizontally for balance.

deadman's float	front float in which the body lies flat on the water, face down, arms stretched forward.
demand valve	also known as a regulator, this is the mechanism on an aqualung which controls the supply of compressed air used by a skindiver.
dribbling	in water polo the method of moving the ball around the pool; the player swims crawl and the ball is carried on the small wave created in front of his face.
drownproofing	survival technique designed for floaters and non-floaters alike; it allows an exhausted swimmer to stay afloat indefinitely while ensuring maximum rest.
dry pass	in water polo a pass in which the ball is thrown over the surface of the water to a stationary player.
eggbeater kick	alternate scissors-like leg kick often used by goalkeepers in water polo.
equalizing	yawning, swallowing or blowing gently through closed nostrils to equalize the pressure in the ears and nose with that of the water.
fireman's lift	method of carrying an unconscious person out of the water so that he is lying over the rescuer's shoulder, one arm and leg held tightly by the rescuer.
flutter kick	the crawl kick in which the legs move up and down alternately from the hips; it is used particularly for swimming with fins when it is a more gentle movement than in the crawl.

freestyle in competition a freestyle event means that a swimmer may use any style of swimming; in a medley event it generally means any stroke other than the butterfly, breaststroke or backstroke; in practice the front crawl is usually chosen.

hang five in surfing this is when a surfer curls one foot over the nose of his surfboard.

hanging ten is when a surfer stands with both feet over the front of his surfboard.

hurdle the final part of a diver's approach to takeoff; consists of a spring up from, and back onto, the board before taking off into a dive.

hyperventilation in underwater swimming the practise of taking too many deep breaths before submerging; it can lead to loss of consciousness as it causes the level of carbon dioxide in the body to drop dangerously.

inward dive swimmer takes off facing the board but enters the water facing away from it.

jackknife position in which the body is bent at the hips but the knees are kept straight.

jellyfish float alternative name for cork float.

layout dive alternative name for straight dive; the body is fully stretched without being bent at knees or hips.

luffing up in windsurfing this is when the mast is inclined aft so that the boom is brought closer in.

mushroom float	alternative name for cork float.
pearling	surfing term meaning a nose dive.
pike	position in which the body is bent at the hips with knees kept straight; also known as jack-knife.
reverse dive	swimmer takes off facing forward but reverses in the air, entering the water facing the board.
rolling pickup	in water polo method of picking up the ball by placing a hand on the top of the ball and rolling it sideways and down so that it can be lifted out of the water.
scissors kick	sideways opening and closing motion of the legs rather like the action of a pair of scissors; used in treading water.
sculling	outward and downward rotation of the hands from the wrists; used in treading water.
split jump	feetfirst entry into shallow water; after an approach run, or from a standing position, the swimmer jumps into the water legs spread forwards and backwards; the legs are closed after entering the water.
stride jump	alternative name for split jump.
treading water	method of staying afloat in a vertical position by moving the legs, and possibly the hands.
wet pass	a pass in water polo in which the ball is thrown to a moving player so that it lands just in front of him.

Index

Accidents 106
Air pressure 95, 96
Amateur Swimming Association 42
Ankle exercise 62
Anoxia 98
Aqualung 93
Armstand dives 61, 84
Artificial respiration 106, 107, 114–115
Atmospheres 96

Back dives 61, 68–69, 70, 71, 84
Backhand shot 141
Backstroke 30–31, 44, 48
Backward fall 99
Ball (water polo) 137, 138, 139
Bends, the 96
Bicycle kick 18
Board exercises 62
Breaststroke 23, 26, 36–37, 44, 50, 109, 113, 138
Breathing 14, 21, 35
Buoyancy 10, 20, 32, 98
Butterfly 23, 44, 50
Butterfly dolphin 26, 40–41

Clothing (inflated) 110–111
Colds 97, 106

Competition diving 80–87
Competition swimming 42–51
Confidence 13, 14
Cook, James 122
Cork float 14
Corkscrew 123
Cousteau, Jacques Yves 90
Cramp 106, 112
Crawl 22, 23, 28, 32–33
Cross-chest tow 113
Cross position 63, 66
Currents 20, 106

Dangers 20, 106
Danger signals 106
Deadman's float 14
Deep-water start 131
Demand valve 90, 93
Display skiing 130, 131
Distortion (underwater) 100
Diving boards 60, 82, 83
Diving practice 69, 72, 75, 77
Diving suits 93
Dog paddle 26, 28–29
Dolphin 121
Dribbling 140
Drowning 106, 112
Drownproofing 110–111
Dry pass 140–141
Dynamics 22–23

Ear plugs 92, 97
Ears 97, 106
Eggbeater kick 138, 139
Emergencies 106, 109, 112, 115
Entry (diving) 61, 87
Equalizing 95, 97
Exercises 150–151
Exhaustion 112

False start 47
Fédération Internationale de Natation Amateur (FINA) 42
Feetfirst entries 87, 108
Finning 94, 98
Fins 92, 99, 122
Fireman's lift 115
Fitness 106, 151
Floating 14–15, 95, 110–111
Floating square 132, 133
Floats 12, 13, 18, 110–111
Flutter kick 33, 94
Forward dive 61, 84
Forward dive, half twist 74
Forward dive with tuck 77
Forward pike 67, 76
Forward 1½ somersault tuck 78
Forward tumble 56
Fouls (water polo) 146–147

Freestyle 44, 48
Frog kick 18
Front crawl 34–35, 48, 138
Front header 65

Gagnan, Emil 90
Gliding 16–17, 30, 37
Goal judges (water polo) 136, 145
Goalkeeping (water polo) 142–143
Goals (water polo) 137
Goggles 92
Goofy foot stance 123

Hand signals 100–101
Hang five 126
Hanging ten 126
Headfirst entries 57, 61, 87, 109
Headgrip 113
Highboards 60, 82, 83
Horse and rider 121
Hurdle positions 66
Hyperventilation 98

Illness 106
In-water aid 115
Inward dive 61, 72–73, 84
Inward dive, pike 73

Jackknife (dive) 61, 76

Jackknife (float) 14
Jellyfish float 14
Judging (diving) 86
Jump entry 99

Knife (underwater) 93, 103

Landing 114
Leapfrog 121
Lifejacket 92, 108
Lifesaving 26, 30, 106, 112–113, 114–115
Lob shot 141
Luffing up 129
Lungs 97, 98

Marine biology 103
Marking 140
Mask 92, 96, 99
Mask clearing 97
Mask squeeze 97
Massed floating 133
Mono skiing 131
Mouth-to-mouth respiration 114, 115
Mushroom float 14

Newton's third law of motion 22
Nitrogen narcosis 96
Nonfloaters 110
Nonswimmers 12, 106, 113, 118
Nose clips 92

Nose ride 126

Officials
  diving 82
  swimming 55
  water polo 136, 144
Olympic events 51, 82, 84–85
Olympic Games 42, 44, 80, 84
Ornamental swimming 132–133
Overconfidence 106

Panic 106, 112, 113
Panic holds 113
Passing 140–141
Pike dive 61, 86
Pike drill 76
Pike float 14
Pearling 132
Plunge dive 58–59
Pool (water polo) 136, 137
Porpoise 121
Posture (diving) 62
Power pull (back crawl) 38
Pressure 96–97, 98
Propulsion 23
Push shot 141

Racing dive 58–59
Referees (water polo) 136, 144
Rescue aids 112
Reverse dive 61, 70–71, 84

Reverse dive, half twist 75
Reverse dive, straight 71
Reverse dive, tuck 77
Reverse somersault,
 straight 79
Rivers 106
Rolling 120, 121
Rolling pickup 138
Rowing 112
Running dive 61, 86

Safety equipment 112
Safety precautions 20, 60,
 92, 106–115
Scissor float 132, 133
Scissors kick 18, 30
Scoring (diving) 87
Scoring (water polo) 143
Sculling 18, 121
Sea 20, 106
Secretaries (water polo)
 136, 145
Shallow water 108
Shooting 141
Side slip 126
Side stroke 30–31, 113
Silvester Brosch method
 115
Simon Says 120, 121
Sinking 98
Skindiving 26, 94, 95, 97
Snorkel 92
Snorkel clearing 97
Snorkeling 94, 98

Somersaults
 diving 78–79
 swimming 120–121
Spearfishing 103
Spearhead principle 47
Spin turn 50, 51
Split jump 108
Springboards 60, 82, 83
Standing dive 61, 86
Standing front jump 63
Starting positions 46–47
Step entry 108
Straight (layout) dive 61
Stride jump 108
Stunts 120–121
Submerging 98, 99, 109
Surface dives 99
Surfboard 127
Surfing 122–127
Survival techniques 110–111
Swan dive 67
Swimming costume 12, 14
Synchronized swimming
 132–133

Tackling 140
Takeoff (diving) 61, 70, 86
Throwing 138
Tides 20, 106
Timekeepers (water polo)
 136, 145
Torch (underwater) 93
Towing 112, 113
Training 150–151

Treading water 18–19, 94, 99
Tricks 120–121
Trudgen 28–29
Tube ride 127
Tuck dive 61, 77, 86
Tuck entry 108
Tumble turn 48–49
Turning 48–49
Turning on the board 69
Twisting action 74
Twist dives 74–75, 84

Underwater archaeology 103
Underwater communication
 100–101
Underwater equipment
 92–93
Underwater photography 103
Underwater skills 94–95
Underwater swimming
 90–103
Underwater torpedo 121

Wading 112
Warming up 150
Water fun 118, 120–121
Water polo 134–147
Water resistance 22–23
Water skiing 130–131
Water skis 130
Weeds 106
Weight belt 93
Wet pass 140, 141
Windsurfing 128–129